11+ Years
in the
Life
of an
Immigrant

11+ Years

in the

Life

of an

Immigrant

JAMES C. STATHIS

iUniverse, Inc.

New York Lincoln Shanghai

11+ Years in the Life of an Immigrant

Copyright © 2006 by James C. Stathis

iUniverse books may be ordered through booksellers or by contacting:

iUniverse
2021 Pine Lake Road, Suite 100
Lincoln, NE 68512
www.iuniverse.com
1-800-Authors (1-800-288-4677)

ISBN-13: 978-0-595-41515-1 (pbk)
ISBN-13: 978-0-595-86538-3 (cloth)
ISBN-13: 978-0-595-85864-4 (ebk)
ISBN-10: 0-595-41515-6 (pbk)
ISBN-10: 0-595-86538-0 (cloth)
ISBN-10: 0-595-85864-3 (ebk)

Printed in the United States of America

This book is dedicated to my family and friends, especially to my beloved wife Alice who stood by me during our struggle with the Immigration and Naturalization Service.

Contents

11+ YEARS
IN THE LIFE OF AN
IMMIGRANT

Last Sunday morning I was watching Senator Lindsey Graham (R-SC) on TV, explaining President Bush's "Immigration Plan," and suddenly it dawned on me that this was the exact path Alice and I followed to become American citizens.

We arrived in New York in October of 1958 and we became American citizens in March of 1970. It took us eleven years and five months to accomplish our dream.

At the time, I was fluent in English, but Alice didn't speak a word of it. A few years ago, she retired as Professor of Mathematics, teaching mathematics and computer science in colleges in New Jersey and Georgia.

I realized that Alice and I are true living examples of the immigration legislation pending in the Senate to solve the problem of the eleven million illegal immigrants living in our country. It appears that the Senate is trying to write legislation that would put new immigrants in the same path. It took us six years to become permanent residents of the United States by obtaining our green cards, and another five years to become American citizens. All in all, eleven plus years.

If there is a message to be conveyed here to every immigrant, it boils down to two basic adjustments: First and foremost learn how to speak English. This can be accomplished by (a) attending night schools; (b) seeking employment with an American firm where the co-workers converse in English; and (©) reading English books in your spare hours. You can find books of your choice in public libraries.

The second adjustment involves attitude. Embrace your new country whole-heartedly by adopting the American culture. Try to Americanize yourself as soon as possible. Become an active member in your community. Speak English at home and make sure your children learn first English and then the language of your native country. Becoming bi-lingual or multi-lingual is an added advantage; however, the dominant language should be decisively English. That is the only way you will succeed in life and in business in your newly adopted country.

Georgia's immigrant population is the fourth largest in the country—33% of the state population. In 2000, 30.7% of the nation's population was repre-sented by immigrants. In 2005, that percentage grew to 35.6%. In other words, during the course of five years, the immigrant population grew by 15%. Some of the targeted states used to be Arizona, California, Florida, Georgia, New York and Texas. Now, immigrants flood all over the country, as far north as Minnesota, South Dakota and Maine.

Millions of American citizens born of immigrant parents have excelled in art, medicine, music, politics and sports. Just to name a few: Tiger Woods (Thai); Super Bowl Champion and MVP Hines Ward (South Korean); legendary tennis champions Pete Sampras (Greek); Ivan Lendl (Czechoslovakian), and Martina Navratilova (Czechoslovakian); one of the wealthiest global investors George Soros (Hungarian); Chairmain of The Red Apple Group and publisher of the *Hellenic Times* John Catsimatidis (Greek); Senator Paul S. Sarbanes (D-MD) (Greek) and many more.

Of course, no one can forget the famous comedian/entertainer, who lived to be 100 years old, Bob Hope (British), and the composer/musician who also lived to be 100 years old, Irving Berlin (Russian), who wrote the lyrics and composed the music to…*God Bless America.*

No doubt, we are a nation of immigrants.

WHAT EVER HAPPENED TO COMMON SENSE AND TELLING THE TRUTH?

I simply cannot take it any more. I've had it up to my neck with lies and distortions coming out of Washington, D.C., the stupid decisions reached by some of our politicians and their inexcusable apologies for their misbehavior. So, I decided to write a book by accentuating the Truth and emphasizing the value and proper guidance by applying Common Sense in our daily decisions.

It is my hope that my grandson William "Bill" Stathis Batty will someday read this book to his children and grandchildren, demonstrating by factual events that once upon a time there were decent and honest people living in this great country of ours called the United States of America.

This morning when I woke up, the first piece of news that caught my eye was Newsweek's apology for their story on alleged desecration. The story goes that an interrogator at the U.S. prison in Guantanamo Bay, Cuba placed the Koran in the washroom in order to unsettle some of the prisoners and ultimately flushed it down the toilet. Now, who on earth in his right mind will flush the holy book down the toilet? Was this act guided by Common Sense? Obviously not. Did it happen as reported? Apparently not, since Newsweek is apologizing for their mistaken story.

Then why on earth a respected magazine like Newsweek went ahead publishing such a story which created massive demonstrations in Afghanistan where at least 15 people died? The President of Pakistan General Pervez Musharaf, an ally of the United States, demanded an investigation and the punishment of those responsible for the desecration. The worst is yet to come. Next week, there will be massive demonstrations by Islamic groups in Muslim countries like Pakistan, Egypt, Malaysia, Iran, Iraq and Turkey. And all this because one irresponsible person failed to seek the Truth behind the story and authorize its publication without due diligence.

One has to be an imbecile to believe that a book can be flushed down the toilet. Physically, it is just not possible. However, let us assume that it could be done. Wasn't there a higher executive at Newsweek who could question the wisdom of such a story being published? What kind of image would it portray about the United States in the Arab world? It makes a lot of Common Sense to question the good, the benefit, the validity and the source of the story, before it is published. One has to be mentally deficient to allow such a fictitious story to be published with no benefit to anyone. To prove my point, here is a survey conducted by AOL the day of the apology. Among 92,079 participants, here are their votes on two key questions:

Do you typically trust the news media?

| No | 84% |
| Yes | 16% |

Where do you get most of your news?

Internet	38%
TV	34%
Newspapers	15%
Radio	12%
Magazines	1%

I would certainly not subscribe to Newsweek in order to keep myself informed about global events. That's plain, simple and pure Common Sense.

CONSCIENCE

Here is an intangible quality that is hard to find nowadays among our leaders, government or corporate. They will say anything and do anything without checking with their conscience. I remember during my military service in the Turkish Army (I was an English interpreter assigned to a Brigadier General) the General used to tell us: "Let your soul guide you to your destination." In English, we have a similar proverb: "Let your conscience be your guide." One has to have principles to abide by in life. One of those principles is a conscientious one. It guides us through the right path. It distinguishes the right from the wrong. It is a faculty which decides upon the moral quality of our actions.

George Washington once said: "Labor to keep alive in your breast that little spark of celestial fire, called conscience."

Unfortunately a great number of our leaders do not interact with this precious principle in their decision making process. Let me cite an example which happened not long ago. A prominent CEO of a major corporation took his wife to a Mediterranean island along with some hundred guests to celebrate her birthday. He charged his corporation millions of dollars to cover the cost of the birthday party. If he had the slightest conscientious principle in his system, it would have alerted him: DON'T. DON'T DO IT. IT IS ILLEGAL. IT IS IMMORAL.

Unfortunately he did it, because he had no conscience to guide him in his decision making process. He was indicted. In his trial, the prosecutor asked him if he had authorized to himself a $25 million loan from the treasury of the corporation. He proudly answered "yes," not only to himself but to the rest of the officers of the corporation. The prosecutor went on asking him if he subsequently had authorized the forgiveness of that loan. Again he answered in the affirmative. Then the prosecutor asked him where was the $25 million bonus he had collected. "I never received a $25 million dollar bonus" was his reply. The prosecutor reminded him that the $25 million bonus was missing from his income tax return and that he was now charged with evasion of taxes, in addition to the multiple charges he was facing. Stupid?…absolutely! Unethical?…surely! Immoral?…no doubt! All these counts of indictment because he had no conscience to guide him through the right path.

This was just one example. Similar unethical and immoral acts are committed every so often by some of our politicians. The irony of the matter is that we, the public, are as guilty as they are, because when we go to the booth to cast our ballot, we do not check with our conscience if we are casting the right ballot for the right candidate.

May God bless General Resit Ertegun's soul. (pronounced Re-SHEET Erte-GOON) I am forever grateful for his valuable teachings.

BRIGADIER GENERAL RESIT ERTEGUN

Supreme Commander of Istanbul

I was very fortunate when I joined the Turkish Army to have been appointed as an English interpreter to Brigadier General Resit Ertegun, Supreme Commander of the city of Istanbul. I was 20 years old. Single. Carefree. I went into the Army as a playboy, but when I came out of it, I was honorably discharged as a very mature young man. What a difference those two years had done to my way of thinking.

When I joined the General's staff, words like determination, perseverance, courage, vision, goals, planning, objectives, foresight, strategy, discipline, were totally abstract and meaningless to me. Surely they were words contained in the dictionary, but not in my faculties. My brain had not embraced them yet, let alone put them into practice. Little did I know then, that in the course of the next two years, I would master the full meaning of each and every word and that they would play a significant role later on in my life.

A few months before my discharge, I had come to realize that I was not serving a general, but a philosopher like Socrates, who was trying to shape up the character of the young people in his staff, preparing them to become self-assured, confident and mature before they were honorably discharged from his command. Although the General was a firm and authoritarian type of commander, he had his soft and compassionate moments, especially when the occasion called for a teaching. He would take the time and with a great deal of patience he would make his point. Then, he would ask one of us to repeat what he had just said, the way we had understood it. If the repetition was not convincing enough to him, he would start all over, until the point was well absorbed into our minds.

Let me cite an example by picking up the word courage. He told us that in order to become courageous the first thing you need to do is to eliminate fear. You accomplish that with discipline and self-assurance. You need to build up your confidence in order to become courageous. He told us that Abraham Lincoln described courage best. He said: "Courage is not the substitute of fear, but the conqueror of fear." And in whatever you courageously engage, make sure you have done the proper planning, you have laid down the right strategy, and you know when and how to strike decisively. That is a courageous act.

The General was a womanizer. His flirtations surrounded mostly the wives of foreign diplomats. I can hardly recall a month going by without attending a cocktail party given by a diplomat—Ambassador, Consul General, Military Attache and the like. Some months were filled up with three to four cocktail parties. The General also hosted two cocktail parties a year, renting the ballrooms of foreign embassies.

His favorite gift to his ladies of preference was a crystal bowl filled with Madeleine chocolates and wrapped around with a big red bow on the top. I lost count of how many crystal bowls I personally delivered.

As a result of his very active social life, the General had a great deal of influence among foreign diplomats, to the point where the Chief of Staff of the Turkish Armed Forces, a four-star general called Sukru Kanatli, often would call my General asking his personal intervention with a given country's ambassador or military attache. The General would promptly accommodate his boss by calling for a luncheon or dinner meeting with the foreign diplomat.

The highlight of my military service, unquestionably, was Field Marshall Montgomery's visit with the General. At the time, Field Marshall Montgomery was the Vice-Chairman of the Eastern-flank of the NATO forces. He was making his tour, visiting the NATO countries under his jurisdiction. Turkey was one of them. His scheduled itinerary called for a visit with the Chief of Staff of the Turkish Armed Forces, General Sukru Kanatli. The following day the Field Marshall was to be given a tour of Istanbul. The British Ambassador had recommended to Field Marshall Montgomery that he pay a visit to General Resit Ertegun. In his words: "It will be worth your time."

We truly rolled out the red carpet for the Field Marshall. The General came out of his office and met the Field Marshall half way down the hallway and accompanied him to his headquarters. Field Marshall Montgomery was treated to a cup of tea with biscuits. I was translating one compliment after another exchanged between the two leaders. The General congratulated Field Marshall Montgomery on his victories in El Al Mein and on D Day. It was a cordial visit which lasted about fifteen minutes.

The day of our discharge was rather formal with mixed emotions. Although we were happy to return to private life, most of us realized that we were losing a great commander, a great teacher and a great mentor. Right there and then, most of us concluded that General Resit Ertegun was an irreplaceable commander.

About six months following my discharge, one nice morning I read in the newspaper that Brigadier General Resit Ertegun was promoted to Major General and he was appointed Supreme Commander of the Bosphorus Straits. This was a strategic post usually given to an admiral. It was the first time that an army general was appointed to the post. It was obvious that my General's exceptional ability for skillful strategy was the main motivator behind his appointment. His headquarters were situated at the end of the Bosphorus Straits leading into the Black Sea. Needless to mention, it was a restricted area. No civilians were allowed to enter.

I picked up the phone to congratulate him on his promotion. He was pleased to hear from me and invited me to have lunch with him. I reminded the General that I was now a civilian and the area was restricted to civilians. He told me not to worry about it. He suggested that I take the ferry boat to the last stop and there would be a PT boat waiting for me there. So I did.

As I disembarked the ferry, my eye caught the PT boat with two sailors standing at attention. I was about 15 or 20 feet away when one of the sailors bent down and rolled a red carpet in front me. I must admit, I was overly impressed. Both sailors saluted their guest. I returned the salute. I saluted the flag and I was on board. During the trip I tried to strike a conversation with the sailors but all I got was "Yes Sir," "No Sir."

The General's office was quite lavish. There were two 12 feet high double wooden doors with two guards standing at each side. The room was humongous with his desk all the way at the end in front of three large windows. As I started walking towards him, the General stood up and walked towards me. We met halfway. I was ready to salute when he extended his hand for a firm shake and immediately hugged me. I must admit, it was both an emotional and a pleasant experience for me. Here was the commander I had served for almost two years, so down to earth and friendly. We talked on a variety of subjects. We had lunch. Freshly caught fish, grilled, with green salad and Turkish delights for dessert, including baklava.

The PT boat was waiting to take me back to the ferry. I must admit, this was the most royal reception and that I have ever been the recipient of. To this date, I cherish the memory of every minute of it.

That was the last time I saw General Resit Ertegun.

Subsequently, I heard that he was promoted to Lieutenant General and retired. He passed away soon following his retirement. It is my assumption that retirement didn't suit him well. For a man who had such an active social life, to retire to nothing is rather depressing.

At any rate, he was a great commander. May God bless his soul.

U. S. PRESIDENTS

I have seen a dozen United States Presidents, beginning with President Truman. In my opinion, two stand head and shoulders above the rest. President Harry S. Truman and President Ronald W. Reagan.

Ironically enough, neither one of them was prepared to become the President of the United States. The first one was a haberdasher from the Midwest who went bankrupt. He subsequently decided to run for the Senate from his home state Missouri and later was picked by President Roosevelt as his running mate during his last term. The latter was an actor in Hollywood who was elected Governor of California before he decided to make a run for the Presidency. Why do I select these two as the best above the rest? Because of their honesty, integrity, Truthfulness and applying Common Sense in their decisions, some of them unprecedented and monumental.

Upon President Roosevelt's death, President Truman was sworn in as the 33rd Chief Commander of the nation, totally unprepared to face the challenges of the day. The war was raging in the Pacific. Casualties were high. Our fleet and the Marines were liberating one island after another in the Pacific, with the Japanese fighting till death. There is a tradition among the Japanese which has prevailed over centuries: "Death in Battle is the Highest Honor." President Truman was not aware of the Manhattan Project when he took office. When he was made aware of the existence of the atomic bomb, he weighed his options. He applied Common Sense in reaching his decision. He authorized the drop of the first atomic bomb in Hiroshima and another in Nagasaki. That forced the Japanese to an unconditional surrender. It is estimated that the dropping of the two atomic bombs saved at least 50,000 American lives, on a conservative estimate, and tens of thousands in wounded Marines. It was an unprecedented move in our modern history.

To this date, some mindless critics count how many Japanese died from the twin atomic bombs, instead of counting how many American lives were saved by shortening the war. They look at the hole, instead of the doughnut. History has already recorded that President Truman was one of the most courageous and patriotic Presidents of the United States.

The site to sign the unconditional surrender was selected to be the Missouri battleship. The Missouri, commonly known as the Big Mo, was sort of President Truman's adopted child. While a Senator, he headed the committee to authorize the building of a big battleship. It was christened by his daughter Margaret. One reporter called it: "Christened by a feisty daughter of a feisty Senator." The Missouri was one of the largest, fastest and most sophisticated battleships of its time.

The Japanese expected a revengeful ceremony. Instead, General McArthur was very magnanimous in declaring the end of the war and wishing peace throughout the world. At the time, I admired him for his noble act in elevating himself above resentment. Later on, however, I detested him for his super ego and his decisions to serve no one but his self-centered personality. Pure selfishness. All actions were motivated to benefit his own welfare and no one else's.

Five years later, President Truman was facing the dilemma of the Korean war. Especially when the Red Army of China had joined the North Koreans in pushing the Allied Forces south. At the time, I was in the Turkish Army serving General Resit Ertegun. Because of his exceptional ability to strategize, the General was considered among the top candidates to be sent to Korea with a brigade of Turkish soldiers to join the Allied Forces. Through his well placed connections in the hierarchy, he managed to substitute his name with that of another Brigadier General who unfortunately died in Korea with his entire brigade. The Turks had lost contact with the Allied Forces and missed the call to withdraw. So when the Allied Forces withdrew south during the night, at dawn the Turks found themselves totally unprotected and all by themselves to fight the surging North Korean troops. They fought valiantly but at the end they succumbed. They were completely massacred.

In as much as President Truman was willing to put an end to the Korean war, General McArthur who was commanding our troops in Korea, was against it. Not only did he disobey President Truman's orders, but he was downright arrogant about it. He didn't hesitate to demonstrate his arrogance publicly either. So President Truman had to reach a decision. Once again, he applied Common Sense and he came up with the one and only practical decision. He fired General McArthur. No other President would have had the courage—let me be more blunt—the guts to fire a five star general. It would have been unthinkable. Nevertheless, President Truman did it and life went on.

One of his great humanitarian achievements was the Marshall Plan which was born out of the Truman Doctrine. Right after World War II, Greece was engaged in an interior civil war which was tearing the country apart. Turkey was threatened with communist insurgents from Russia. President Truman provided General Papagos of the Greek Army with sufficient support to put the rebels down and form a stable government. The Marshall Plan was the right prescription to lift the economies of Greece, Turkey and all the Mediterranean countries which had suffered from World War II.

President Truman was an honest and simple man. His famous slogan "The buck stops here" is still used by many politicians today. He was also the founder of the United Nations and the North Atlantic Treaty Organization, both providing an umbrella of alliances against Soviet threat. No doubt, he was a visionary leader.

When Ronald Reagan became the 40th President of the United States, the country was in a mess. We had the personnel of the American Embassy in Teheran held hostage for 444 days, one of the many fumbles of the Carter administration. President Carter's ignorance in foreign affairs caused him one trouble after another. He lacked both the experience and the savvy how to deal with foreign countries. He had no capacity to comprehend the different cultures in different countries. He was the principal cause of the downfall of Shah Pehlevi, the ruler of Iran, a strong ally of the United States. Shah Pehlevi was replaced by Ayatollah Khomeni, a fanatic religious head who took the country 100 years back overnight.

Teheran was a cosmopolitan capital where its citizens enjoyed freedom unparallel to its neighbors. Overnight, things changed. Women were forced to change their attire. No more western wardrobes. They were forced to cover their head and wear a veil.

Foreign languages were removed from the curriculum and the principal book in elementary schools became the Koran. Trips abroad were forbidden.

When President Reagan took office, the economy was in a mess. Interest rates were 17% and rising. The housing industry was experiencing the lowest level of sales because of the lack of mortgages. Gasoline prices were rising and there were long lines in gas stations. Inflation was galloping in double digits. What is worth mentioning here for my readers is that when President Carter was running against President Ford, he had invented the "misery index" which at the time stood at 10.

Unemployment plus inflation equaled the "misery index." During his four year term, President Carter's "misery index" had doubled.

Needless to mention that President Reagan had his hands full in addressing each and every one of these serious problems he had inherited from the previous administration. To top it off, early on during his Presidency the Air Traffic Controllers Union threatened a strike unless their wage and benefits demands were met. This would have been a catastrophic blow to the economy. Not only airports would have been shut down, airlines would have been grounded, the tourist industry would have come to a halt, hotels and resorts would have suffered immensely. With lightening speed President Reagan abolished the union and averted a catastrophe. It took courage and a principle of conscience to act so decisively.

In October 1983, during the first term of his presidency, the Organization of Eastern Caribbean States asked President Reagan to intervene militarily on the island of Grenada whose Prime Minister Maurice Bishop had been executed by radical leftists committed to Marxism and supported by Fidel Castro of Cuba. Neighbors of Grenada, like Antigua, Barbados, Dominica, St. Lucia and St. Vincent had warned our government that there was a Cuban-sponsored military buildup taking place in Grenada. They were willing to dislodge the radicals but they did not have the power. They were asking the United States to intervene.

There were 800 American students in Grenada attending medical school at St. George's University Medical School. It was of paramount importance that the invasion was done secretly and promptly before the American students fell hostages in the hands of the leftists guerillas. Grenada was independent, under the auspices and protection of the United Kingdom. There was no time to advise Margaret Thatcher, the then Prime Minister of Great Britain, of the impending invasion. President Reagan gave the go ahead and the whole operation was executed swiftly and successfully, bringing home the 800 American students. One marine died during the invasion.

The very next morning President Reagan was informed by the Secretary of State Schultz of the tragic death of 241 marines in Beirut when a suicide bomber drove a truckload of dynamite smashing it in the barracks of the Beirut Airport where all 241 marines were asleep. Once again, he had an urgent case in his hands that called for decisive action. After calling for an emergency session of the Congress, a combined force consisting of the Air Force, the Navy and the Marines was dispatched to Beirut to take control of the situation.

To President Reagan's credit, neither Grenada nor Beirut ended up becoming another Vietnam. Following the success of several operations, he withdrew our troops and brought them home. In fact, it was President Reagan's administration that had adopted a set of principles to guide future presidents on the application of military force abroad. These principles were:

1. No U.S. forces should be committed overseas unless American lives or the national interest is at task.

2. Clearly defined and realistic objectives. When the mission is accomplished, U.S. troops should return home immediately.

3. Must have the support of the American people and the Congress.

4. Only as a last resort, when no other choice is available.

Most unfortunately, all of the above principles were grossly violated when President George W. Bush elected to invade Iraq.

Finally, President Reagan's greatest success story was his negotiations with the Soviet Union. First he built up our armed forces and then started negotiating from strength. He was the only President who had the courage to call the

Soviet Union the "Evil Empire." He called it as he saw it. No fancy words or phony compliments. He survived Leonid Breznev, Yuri Andrepov and Konstantin Chernenko. On March 11, 1985, upon Chernenko's death Mikhail Gorbachev took over as the new head of the Soviet Union.

Gorbacev was a different leader. He had an open mind and he was ready to negotiate. He was personable and he radiated trust. During the ensuing three and half years President Reagan and Mikhail Gorbacev developed a very close relationship. They trusted each other. At the end they became very close friends. It was Mikhail Gorbacev who brought reform to the Soviet Union. He stopped spending zillions of rubles to build up nuclear weapons. Instead, he tried to revive the collapsing economy. The collapse of the Berlin wall was indicative of the changes taking place in the Soviet Union. He was a man of renaissance. The Soviet Union had not seen such rejuvenation in the previous six decades.

President Reagan in his memoirs spoke very fondly of Mikhail Gorbacev. He said: "…whatever his reasons, Gorbacev had the intelligence to admit Communism was not working, the courage to battle for change, and ultimately, the wisdom to introduce the beginnings of democracy, individual freedom, and free enterprise."

Mighty high praise coming from the leader of the most powerful nation on earth.

It is my understanding that Mr. Gorbacev is now a resident of the City of New York and he is teaching Political Science at Columbia University. I would pay a premium to become a student in his class.

His Eminence Archbishop Demetrios, Archbishop of America and Exarch of Ecumenical Patriarch Bartholomew, announced this week that Mikhail Gorbachev will be honored with the 2005 Athenagoras Human Rights Award to be presented to him at the New York Hilton Hotel on October 22nd. Former recipients of this honor are Presidents Jimmy Carter and George Herbert Walker Bush, Mother Theresa, Archbishop Desmond Tutu and the late Archbishop Iakovos.

In recognition of his outstanding services as a great reformer and world political leader, Mikhail Gorbachev was awarded the Nobel Peace Prize on October 15, 1990.

Mr. Gorbachev has received scores of other awards and honors, including the Gold Medal from the Prometheus National Technological University of Athens and the Gold Medal of Thessaloniki, both in 1993, the Martin Luther King International Peace Award in 1991, and the Sir Winston Churchill Award to recognize his contribution to peace in the Middle East in 1993.

The world salutes this great mind of reform.

HONEYMOON TRIP

Alice and I were married on September 22, 1957. I had promised her a honeymoon trip around the world. We knew in advance that it would take some time before we embarked on our honeymoon trip because of the long delays in obtaining our passports and the different visas required from the countries we intended to visit.

So, following our wedding we took a short honeymoon trip for a week in Bursa, known for its thermal hot springs and its majestic views of green valleys and mountains.

Upon our return home, the first thing I did was to apply for our passports. At the time, Turkey was suffering from foreign exchange shortages. American dollars, British pounds and German marks were scarce. The Ministry of Justice which was issuing the passports, used to issue a $200.00 allowance for each passport recipient. There was, therefore, a significant delay in the issuance of passports depending on the in-flow of foreign exchange.

Finally, after almost a year's delay, we managed to obtain our passports and all the required visas from the respective foreign embassies. At that point, I bought two round trip tickets around the world from Pan American Airways, with open dates and cities. It cost me $3,000.00—in reality twice that amount—because I had to buy the dollars on the black market. Pan Am wouldn't issue the tickets unless they were paid in U.S. currency. And off we went.

By the time we reached Rome, Italy we discovered that Alice was pregnant. When we arrived in Zurich, Switzerland the doctors told us that we had to curtail our trip because Alice was risking losing the baby with this frequent and hectic traveling. Our schedule called for Germany, France, Spain, Portugal, Sweden, Denmark, Norway, United States, Japan, Hong Kong, Thailand and back home. So we decided to by-pass all the European and Scandinavian countries and head on straight to New York where we could wait until the baby was born and then continue on the rest of our trip.

On October 4, 1958 we arrived in New York at the John F. Kennedy airport (then known as Idlewild). We had reservations at the Broadway Hotel on Broadway and 96th Street. We spent the next two months visiting New York City and spending our money. We had never seen so many theaters, cinemas, department stores within a few miles radius. When our money was exhausted, we felt it was time to move out of the hotel and try to rent a furnished room in a house which would have been less costly. Someone suggested that Brooklyn had some nice communities where we could find a furnished room at reasonable rates and live along with nice families.

So we took the subway and off we went to Brooklyn searching for a furnished room.

By sheer luck, we found this lovely Jewish family in Bensonhurst who were willing to rent us a furnished room in their house. They were Saphardic Jews from Greece.

Mrs. Sarah Barkey spoke Greek which was very helpful for Alice. Mr. Bert Barkey was a retired executive from Paramount Pictures. Their children were grown up and out of the house. It was Mr. & Mrs. Barkey living all by themselves. They welcomed us with open arms as if we were their own children.

It was before the Christmas holidays that I decided it was time for me to find a job because the baby wasn't due for another month and we were down to our last dollar. So, I applied for a Social Security card (a gross violation of the immigration laws for someone who is in the country on a visitor's visa), got the New York Times and went though the classified ads. I responded to a blind ad which turned out to be the New York Life Insurance Company. After extensive tests, I was offered a position as an agent, selling life insurance, with a starting salary of $480.00 per month. In reality it was a draw versus commissions. I had to make enough sales so my earned commission would equal or exceed the $480.00 monthly. Mind you, I had never sold anything in my life. Nevertheless, on December 29, 1958 I was employed as an agent by New

York Life which turned out to be another gross violation of the immigration laws since I had secured employment on a visitor's visa.

On January 17, 1959 our daughter Maria was born. She was a beautiful baby. We were all excited with the new arrival in the family. The delivery took place at St. Joseph's Hospital in Patterson, New Jersey. Why so far from Brooklyn? The answer is twofold. First, I was flat broke and had not received my first monthly pay check from New York Life. Therefore, I couldn't afford to pay an obstetrician nor a hospital for the delivery. Second, Alice and I had a childhood friend from Istanbul by the name of Basil Amfilohiades. Following his graduation from medical school, Dr. Basil Amfilo came to the States and he was doing his residency as an anesthesiologist at St. Joseph's Hospital in Patterson, NJ. Our parents communicated with each other in Istanbul and notified Basil of our dilemma. Dr. Amfilo arranged everything at St. Joseph's Hospital to have the delivery made absolutely gratis. Not only that, but the nuns had offered me a free room and board for the three days that Alice and Maria were kept at the hospital. The British have a wonderful proverb: "A friend in need, is a friend indeed." That is the kind of friend Basil has been to Alice and myself.

I was doing quite well selling life insurance. I was validating my salary and building up a surplus. The secret in that business as in any selling job is prospecting. Have enough customers to see everyday so that the law of averages can work on your behalf. Alice had helped me in jotting down Greek names from the Brooklyn telephone directory whom I called and made appointments to visit with. By this time, some of my General's teachings started coming into play. Determination, planning, strategy, goals. These were some of the intangibles I started employing in my business. The surplus in my account helped me buy our first car. It was a used 1957 DeSoto. It helped me cover my appointments faster.

During the spring of 1959 we discovered that Alice was pregnant with our second child. We were both excited about the prospects of having a second child in the family. Our excitement was slightly dampened by a letter we had received from the Immigration and Naturalization Service (INS) inviting me to a hearing in their downtown Manhattan office. No specifics were mentioned in the letter, other than that if I wished I could be accompanied by my attorney.

Dean was born on December 29, 1959. He was a slim, tall boy. He was born at St. Joseph's Hospital in Patterson, NJ. We had purposely selected the same hospital again. I was gainfully employed this time, and we were in a position to pay. This was our way of reciprocating for the kind accommodations the nuns had extended to both of us. Dr. Amfilo was instrumental again in reducing both the obstetrician's and the hospital's bills. Subsequently, Dr. Amfilo became Dean's godfather by baptizing him in the spring of 1960. Dean's middle name is Basil.

Dean Basil Stathis. He is now a practicing attorney in Atlanta, Georgia.

IMMIGRATION AND NATURALIZATION SERVICE (INS)

The INS people are a special breed of people. I guess they have to be, since they are dealing with different nationalities and cultures.

I didn't make much of the hearing letter. I went there by myself on the scheduled time. Right away, I was hit with a barrage of violations. I do not remember all of them. They must have been about a dozen. The ones that stuck into my mind were: (1) Failure to renew our expired visa to enter the United States. (2) Failure to notify the INS of our changing address. (3) Applying for a Social Security card on a visitor's visa. (4) Securing employment on a visitor's visa. (5) Failure to notify my employer that I was a tourist, visiting the United States on a visitor's visa. (6) Failure to notify my employer that I did not possess a Green Card. (7) Registering a motor vehicle under a different address on an expired visa. And many more which I couldn't remember. Bottom line: I was given 15 days for voluntary departure, otherwise we were facing deportation.

At this point, I knew we were in trouble. I needed the counseling of a good INS attorney. I had become a member of the Hellenic Society of Constantinople, a non-profit civic group composed of Greek-Americans who were born in Istanbul, Turkey. The President of the Society was a dentist who was residing in Central Park South, the district of Congressman John V. Lindsay. (R-NY). He volunteered to ask Congressman Lindsay for his assistance. Sure enough, he managed to get an appointment a couple of weeks down the road when Congressman Lindsay was going to be in town.

Meantime, I was referred to attorney Eugene Rossides who was very influential in high Republican circles. He was close to Senator Jacob Javitz (R-NY) and to Governor Nelson Rockefeller. When I met Gene in his office on Park Avenue he told me that I was coming to him five minutes before midnight—midnight signifying disaster. He told me that he was not an INS attorney, but he was going to put together a team of the best legal minds and he was going to lead the charge. It was going to be a bitter fight and the odds were not in our favor. The alternative was to pack up and leave.

Mesmerized by the immensity of the problem, I sat there in the chair weighing my options. To tell Alice to pack up in her condition, almost three months pregnant, pick up our one-year old daughter Maria and return to Turkey was unacceptable The one and only practical alternative was to fight. And if we didn't succeed, we would have returned to Istanbul anyway. All of a sudden, my General's teachings came into focus. He used to tell us: "You don't fool around with your enemy. You don't entertain your enemy. You simply kill your enemy, so that he will not be able to come back and hurt you again." INS was my enemy. In this fight I had to kill my enemy.

To succeed in my mission, I had to be courageous and determined. I had to have a plan backed up by good fighters (Gene and his team of lawyers). We had to have a strategy that would lead us to victory. Senator Javitz, Governor Rockefeller and Congressman Lindsay were the key elements. Perseverance, discipline, vision with a positive attitude and unyielding determination were the qualities that would elevate me to victory in this fight.

Oh, I wished General Resit Ertegun were here with me, observing my fight, seeing how well I would execute his teachings, observing how well he had prepared me for the fight of my life and that of my growing family. Well planned attacks with precise and decisive blows to the heart, killing the enemy once and for all. I was already dreaming of the day Alice and I would become citizens of this great country of ours.

Eleanor Roosevelt once said: "The future belongs to those who believe in the beauty of their dreams".

My thoughts were interrupted with Gene asking me to show financial statements and resources because this fight was going to cost me tens of thousands of dollars.

I looked Gene straight in the eye and told him to forget about financial statements and resources because there were none. If he had asked me for just a $100 bill, I wouldn't be able to hand it to him. But, I told him, I knew how to earn money. If we could make an arrangement where I could pay his fees on monthly installments, then I would be willing to shake his hand. And I extended my hand for a handshake. "$2,000.00 a month would do" was his answer as he shook my hand. I was frozen. I stood there like a dummy starring at Gene. I was accustomed to validating my salary of $480.00 per month. Now, I had to earn in excess of $2,500.00 every month in order to keep my commitment to Gene and New York Life. "It's a deal", I said. I told Gene that Alice and I were placing our faith in him that he would win this fight for us. In return he was placing his faith in me that I would honor my commitment in paying his fees.

When I went home and told Alice the commitment that I had made to Gene, in a way she was happy that we were staying in the United States and ultimately becoming American citizens, but she was terribly concerned how was I going to keep on earning $2,500.00 every month, consecutively, until the fight was won. I told her that I didn't have an answer right then and there, but I would figure out a way. It has been said:

"When there is a will, there is a way".

The first thing we did, we cashed in the unused portion of our Pan Am ticket which provided us with the first installment of $2,000.00 to Gene. More importantly, it was a psychological reinforcement that we were now determined to fight and stay, because we had no means of transportation back to Istanbul

VISUALIZING THE FUTURE

The General, among his many teachings, used to train us to foresee the future. He used calling it "Visualizing the Future." He would ask us to elevate ourselves by stepping on our toes. Then he would ask: "How do you feel?" The usual answer was that we felt a few centimeters taller. In as much as he agreed with our answers, he would state that in essence we had turned the switch "on" with our faculties. We were now communicating with our faculties. And the best way to do that was to repeat as frequently as we could, a message relating to a future event.

Example: "How am I going to score a goal in next month's soccer game?" or "How am I going to buy that bicycle?" The message needed to be short and concise. Unaltered. Repeated always precisely in the same manner. Repeated morning, noon and night every day. And ultimately, our faculties will provide us with the answer before the day of the event.

There were a few among us who had trepidations playing the game and attempting to communicate with our brain. The General, sensing the apprehension, would not ask us to practice it in his presence. But occasionally, he would bring up the subject of "Visualizing the Future" and emphasize its value.

At New York Life, in the agency, million-dollar-producers had their private offices. The rest shared offices with another agent. I shared my office with Leonard Isaacson who was also a rookie like myself. He had joined New York Life a few months before I did. Len was a delightful chap with a tremendous sense of humor. We turned out to be two good friends. Alice and I have very fond memories from this long standing friendship which we cherish for the past forty seven years.

All the way in the back of the agency, there was a large room which housed five or six semi-retired senior agents. They would usually come around 10:00 o'clock in the morning, have their coffee, exchange some war stories, read their mail, make some phone calls and by noon-time leave for their homes. Their main income was derived from renewal commissions on hundreds of policies that they had sold in previous years. Occasionally, they would make a new sale to one of their old clients. I maintained a good relationship with them and always showed the proper respect to each and everyone of them. The most senior agent was Mr. Schuller.

Confronted with a very heavy financial commitment to Gene, I decided to practice the General's "Visualizing the Future." I phrased it: "How am I going to pay $2,000 to Gene?" Kept on repeating it every morning, noon and night and in between. I do not recall exactly how many days it took, but one night I dreamed the agency, the large room and Mr. Schuller asking me: "How can I help you?" I woke up with full enthusiasm, my emotions thrilled to zenith, because I had just discovered the solution to my problem.

The next morning I ran straight into my manager's office. Marvin L. Carlton was a shrewd manager who had the ability to skillfully derive the very maximum out of every agent. He did it with motivation, he did it by touching your pride, he did it with inspiration, he had a dozen tricks up his sleeve. Marv was very familiar with my situation and he was eager to help me out.

I explained to Marv my strategic plan to earn more than $2,500.00 of commissions every month, consistently, and I needed his approval and cooperation. I was going to hire a secretary who would spend five hours on the phone every day making appointments. I would then distribute the leads among the senior agents and ask them to go out and cover those appointments. On every sale, we would share the earned commissions 50-50. I would go one step further, I would let them keep the credit 100% to themselves, thus qualifying for club status. At New York Life, there were three clubs: Star Club, for those who earned more than $7,500.00 in first-year commissions; Top Club, $15,000.00 and President's Club $25,000.00. President's Council $50,000.00 and over. I would simply collect my 50% in cash from them. I would also throw in a bonus: Any referrals they obtained from the new client, they could keep for themselves.

Marv thought I was a genius. Marv's compensation was based on production. Right away, he could see the multiple benefits to himself. Additional benefits on increased production over the year before. Extra incentives on the number of club qualifiers. More incentives on the increase of club qualifiers over the year before. Additional incentives on the increase of the quality of club qualifiers. Not only did he approve my plan, but he volunteered to announce it jointly to the senior agents. With the exception of one senior agent whose health was failing, the rest embraced the plan enthusiastically. Not only could they see the extra revenue coming in to them, but deep down they wanted to help me out, especially Mr. Schuller, who had offered to write to his Congressman and ask him to intervene on my behalf. I thanked him and asked him not to, because that would have presented a conflict to Congressman Lindsay's efforts.

Now I had a team of five senior agents, plus myself six, working feverishly to earn the maximum amount of commissions every month. I had no problem in meeting my financial commitments to Gene, to New York Life and to my family. In the meantime, I had accelerated my training courses with New York Life. I was taking now Advanced Business Life Insurance courses which enabled me to visit with businesspeople during the day and discuss Partnership Insurance, Redemption Stock Agreements, Deferred Compensation for Executives, Pension Plans, Estate Planning and more. Whichever seemed to be appropriate to cover the financial needs of the particular businessman I was visiting.

Rep. JOHN V. LINDSAY (R-NY)
86th United States Congress
Second Session

The day of the appointment, Stavros Stavropoulos, the dentist, Eugene Rossides and his entourage of three attorneys, all of us went to visit Congressman John V. Lindsay. I was thankful to Stavros for having secured the appointment for us. While waiting in the reception area of the Congressman's office, one of the attorney's tried to fix my tie. Foolishly, I pushed him aside and said: "What's the big deal? I'm going to meet a Congressman." Gene jumped on me instantly, grabbed me by the arm, and in a very firm tone of voice told me: "You're about to meet the future President of the United States." Wow! I was flabbergasted.

This is how high Congressman Lindsay's star was rising. The Republican party was grooming him as their prime candidate to challenge President John F. Kennedy in his 1964 re-election bid. Of course, as we all know, President John F. Kennedy's assassination in November of 1963 altered the course of events.

When we entered Congressman's Lindsay's office I was overwhelmed by his personality. He was a tall (6' 5" or 6' 6") handsome young man. He was wearing a double-breasted suit, with white shirt and a multi-colored striped tie. Truly debonair. He had a captivating smile with a flair of charm. He extended his hand. We shook hands and he congratulated me for having become a father. He assured me that he was going to take care of me and my family. I was speechless. I hardly mustered the strength to say: "Thank you, Sir." He turned to Gene and told him that his strategy was to introduce a private bill in

the Congress which when approved, would render to Alice and myself permanent residency in the United States. Gene reminded Congressman Lindsay
that the time granted to us by INS for voluntary departure had already
expired. The Congressman's response was: "Don't worry about that. I'll take
care of it."

Indeed, the following week, Congressman Lindsay introduced private bill
HR3113 in the 86th Congress, second session, requesting that Alice and I be
granted the status of permanent residents of the United States. At this point,
INS had to put a halt to deportation proceedings which had already been
commenced, pending the outcome of the bill. That took a lot of pressure off
me and Alice. In fact, we moved out of Mr. & Mrs. Barkey's apartment and
we rented our own one-bedroom apartment in the same neighborhood. With
the anticipated arrival of the second baby, we needed the space.

To show my gratitude to Congressman Lindsay, I volunteered to campaign
for his re-election in November of 1960. Both he and Senator Javitz were running for re-election. Incidentally, both of them used to win by a landslide.
Mind you, New York City traditionally votes for Democratic candidates. Yet,
here there were two Republican politicians who were unbeatable.

Unfortunately, our private bill never made it to the floor for a vote. It was
defeated at the Judiciary Committee whose Chairman Congressman Powell
from Philadelphia, I was told, was a very prejudicial person. He liked blonde
hair and blue eyes. He approved petitions from the Scandinavian countries,
Germany, England and Ireland. The rest were hardly approved. I'm sure when
he took a look at our papers, born in Istanbul, Turkey, one cannot find light
complexion from people born in Turkey.

In about a week's time, I received a letter from INS giving us thirty days for
voluntary departure, otherwise we were placed again under deportation. For
the benefit of my readers, once a person is deported from the United States, he
or she can never reenter the country under any status.

In spite of the bad news, Eugene Rossides told me that nothing was lost. We
were back to square one. This time he was going to ask Senator Javitz to intervene on our behalf.

Unfortunately the Senator was busy with his re-election campaign. The thirty-day deadline given to us by INS had expired and once again we found ourselves facing deportation. Gene, at this point, decided to file a petition requesting an extension on our voluntary departure deadline. He knew in advance that the request was going to be denied by the judge. This was a tactic of delay, freezing the deportation proceedings, pending the judge's final decision. As expected, the request was denied. Gene kept Senator Javitz abreast of the developing events and the imminent danger of being deported by INS at any moment.

As soon as the petition was denied, in a matter of days, we received a letter from INS informing us that we would be deported the following Tuesday with a Turkish cargo vessel docked at the 57th Street Pier in Manhattan. At this point, I must admit, I thought that we were losing the fight and that we had exhausted practically all of our options. Not according to Gene. He invited me into his office and laid down his strategy for the following Tuesday.

First he assured me that he had Senator Javitz's promise that the Senator was going to introduce a bill through the Senate as soon as possible. Although no date was set, he reaffirmed his faith in Senator Javitz. He said he was a man of integrity and had never failed to uphold his promise. As far as Tuesday was concerned, he said we should be ready to be accompanied by two INS officers to the pier. Each one of us should be holding tight one of our kids. The kids could not be deported because they were American citizens. They were going to be placed in an orphanage. The INS officers would try to extract the kids from our arms. Gene would have the press waiting in the docks to take pictures of our struggle with the INS officers.

In addition, Gene had made arrangements with the New York Telegraph, an afternoon newspaper, to hold the front page blank, waiting for the press pictures from the pier to be printed on the front page. At this point, with a knot on my throat, I asked Gene what if something went wrong. Alice and I would be on board the cargo vessel without the kids. His answer was: "There is no room for 'ifs' or 'buts.' This is our final stand. A lot of money and time has been invested into this plan. It's got to work."

Sure enough, early Tuesday morning two INS officers showed up and asked us if were ready to be deported. "Sure," I said with a smile. They looked at each other. Usually, they know from experience, that there are tears, cries and all kinds of hysteria when they try to deport people. Here, they had two adults all dressed up with kids bundled up, ready to go. "Where is your luggage?" one of the officers asked. "We have none" I said. "We donated everything to charities." They looked at each other again. They almost had sensed that something wasn't right. One of the officers asked me if he could use our phone. I said: "Sure." He called (probably the INS headquarters) and spoke for a few minutes in a low key voice. "We're going to wait for a few minutes. I'm expecting a phone call," he said. It only took a few minutes until the phone rang. He didn't even allow me to answer. He picked it up himself. We couldn't hear what was said. But we heard clearly and with a great degree of relief what the INS officer told us: "Your deportation has been postponed. You'll receive a letter to that effect." They opened the door and left.

Alice and I literally collapsed on the couch. After taking a deep breath, we hugged and kissed each other. We knew that our strategy had worked. According to Gene, INS had called the pier, and when they found out that the press was there waiting, they decided to postpone. They couldn't afford the negative publicity.

That afternoon, the New York Telegraph hit the stands more than an hour late. I was billed $1,445.00 for overtime pay to the press, the truck drivers and the delivery men. A lot of money, but it was worth every penny of it.

Two days later, we received a letter from INS informing us that our deportation proceedings had been postponed for a couple of weeks. We were going to be notified of the exact day and means of transportation. That was the last letter we ever received from INS. The next mailing we received from INS were our two green cards, since we were now permanent residents of the United States, thanks to Senator Jacob Javitz who had introduced a bill through the Senate on a sixth preference, which was approved, sent to the Congress and this time passed the Judiciary Committee.

It was an ordeal. Six years of struggle. But the end was an elated satisfaction. Granting Alice and I and the kids a new life in a new country. We have a lot of people to thank, especially Gene and his team, Congressman Lindsay, Senator Javitz and Governor Rockefeller who was influential behind the scenes.

I don't want to forget my colleagues at New York Life, Marv Carlton, and many friends who stood by during our troublesome days.

When I visited Gene in his office for the last time to settle my account, I asked him: "How much more do I owe you?" "Nothing" was his answer. "You have paid enough." He was a gentleman. Once again, I thanked him for his brilliant strategy and for his unyielding determination. He fought till his last ounce of courage.

To this date, Alice and I have never sat down to calculate how much money we had spent during our struggle to become permanent residents of the United States. I know that it is over six figures. But whatever the final figure was, it was worth every penny of it. One does not put a price for living, free, in one of the greatest countries on earth.

The next step was to become American citizens. For that honor, we had to wait for five years before we could file our petition for citizenship.

LINCOLN NATIONAL LIFE INSURANCE CO., OF NEW YORK

A wholly owned subsidiary of
LINCOLN NATIONAL LIFE
INSURANCE COMPANY
Ft. Wayne, Indiana.

Lincoln National of Ft. Wayne, Indiana is an old, reputable company, ranking among the top ten life insurance companies in the United States. They operate in all 49 states except New York. The reason is that the New York State Insurance Commissioner imposes uniformity on all companies licensed to do business in New York. They need to pay the same rate of commissions in all 49 states as they do in New York. They need to offer the same portfolio of policies in all 49 states as they do in New York.

Lincoln National for years has been paying commissions as high as 70% of first-year premiums to its top producers. The New York State Insurance Commissioner limits the rate of first-year commissions to 55%. Lincoln National was not willing to alter their method of compensation, for the sake of doing business in New York State. So for years they had stayed out of the New York market. Finally, in the early sixties, they created a wholly owned subsidiary, Lincoln National Life Insurance Company of New York, licensed to conduct business only in the state of New York. In this manner, they not only penetrated the New York market, but the parent company retained its competitive edge in the remaining 49 states by not altering any method of their operations. It was a win-win situation, except for the New York State Insurance Commissioner who was complaining that the name of the subsidiary should be changed to any name other than Lincoln.

In 1964 I received an unusually attractive offer from Lincoln National of New York.

They wanted me to start an agency from scratch for them in Brooklyn, New York. They offered me a guaranteed salary of $50,000.00 per year for two years and thereafter my compensation would be based on production, with several incentives, similar to that of Marv Carlton. In addition, they would reimburse me 100% for all business-related expenses. I was in a dilemma. I didn't want to leave New York Life because they had been very good to me. On the other hand, this kind of offer, which had tremendous potential for growth, comes only once in a lifetime. Quite reluctantly, I submitted my resignation to New York Life. Needless to mention, Marv Carlton was very upset. At the last minute, he offered me an Assistant Manager's position to dissuade me from accepting Lincoln's offer.

The first thing I did was to rent 1,000 square feet of office space with an option to acquire an additional 4,000 square feet in a year's time. I was projecting growth, but I didn't want to overburden Lincoln initially with a heavy rent roll. The next thing I did was to hire a competent secretary. And then I approached my friend Leonard Isaacson and offered him an Assistant Manager's position.

Before talking to Len, I called Marv Carlton and asked for his permission to talk to Len. Once again, he was upset but nevertheless he allowed me to talk to Len with the understanding that I would not approach another associate of his. I gave him my word and I kept it, even though a number of my former New York Life colleagues approached me directly to join my agency.

Starting a scratch agency is a very tough job. It requires hard work, total dedication and long hours. Certain things have to be done at a certain time, regardless if you have the time, the energy or the inclination to do them. They've got to be done. Period. Thank God, Len and I were on the same wavelength. Neither one of us complained about our exhaustive schedule.

Meantime Alice and I had bought a house in Washington Township, New Jersey.

Alice did the hunting, selection, closing, furnishings, etc. I used to put in 14 to 16 hours a day. I barely had time left to come home and go to sleep. The decision to buy a house in a suburbia was Alice's. It was smart, because the children were approaching kindergarten and we had to think ahead to their schooling. The house was lovely, a three-bedroom, 2-bath, split-level built on top of a hill on three quarters of an acre. Fully landscaped. There was a lot of lawn to mow, but I didn't mind doing it during the weekends, because I used that time to do my mental planning for the following week's activities. Later on, when Dean grew up, he would give me a hand.

Our first year was a success beyond our expectations. We exceeded every goal we had set for production, recruiting and cost effectiveness. We acquired the additional 4,000 square feet and we were in need now of an additional secretary and an additional Assistant Manager. He ended up being Albert Castano from Mutual of New York. Al was a prolific producer, selling over 100 policies per year.

Both Len and I had the schooling of Marv Carlton. We were inspiring our agents to maximize their production, to keep up with their education and self-development and as an ultimate goal to improve the standard of living of their families. It worked magnificently.

I had promised Len that I was going to support his promotion to become General Manager of his own agency. On every occasion that I had, I put a good word for him with my Vice President in Charge of Agencies. Finally, three years to the date after he joined me, Len was appointed General Manager of the Queens agency.

Both our families were excited with his promotion. By this time Len had divorced his first wife Carol and he had married Diane, a delightful young lady who lived a little further north of Washington Township. By this time the Brooklyn agency was leading the Company year after year, and we kept on winning the President's Trophy every year as the leading agency.

After two successful years as the Queens Agency's General Manager, Len Isaacson was promoted to Director of Agencies and moved to the Home

Office. He was now my boss. Meantime, my agency kept on growing with new agents coming on board. At this point, the agency had acquired an international flavor. I had six Hispanic agents one each from: Panama, Argentina, Spain and the Dominican Republic and two from Puerto Rico. Two Greek-American agents. One of them, Andrew Koinoglou had joined us from State Mutual Life Insurance Co. Andy was an exceptional individual, very loyal and dedicated family man. He stayed with me all the way till the end of my career. We also had one Persian, one Hungarian, two Israelis, two Jewish-Americans, two African-Americans and five Americans.

The New York State Insurance Commissioner's Office demands that a newly created life insurance company be audited every three years. On every audit, the Commissioner's examiners demanded that the parent company invest additional resources, anywhere from $1 million to $3 million to cover the reserves of the fast-growing subsidiary. The parent company accommodated every demand every three years. At the same time, the Commissioner was renewing his complaint that the subsidiary should be operating under a different name than Lincoln.

The parent company was ignoring at the complaint.

Finally, in 1975 the conflict came to explode. When the examiners demanded additional resources to be invested, the board of directors of the parent company decided to close shop in New York and get out of the New York market. At that point Lincoln National of New York had 32 agencies across the state. At the stroke of the pen, thousands of agents and 32 General Managers were terminated with two weeks' severance pay. My eleven-year successful career came to a sudden halt. Eight of those eleven years my agency had led the company. My agents were in shock. They didn't know what to do. Some of them I placed them with New England Life. Some of them I placed with New York Life. The rest decided to stay with me and follow me into my next career. One of them was Andy Koinoglou.

The termination news came at the most inappropriate moment. Alice, the kids and I were vacationing up north in Maine. Dr. Basil Amfilo, who in the meantime had been married to Sophie, a fine and beautiful young lady from Verona, New Jersey, owned a summer house on Lake Sabago. I was swimming in the lake when I heard Alice calling me to come back because Len Isaacson was on the phone. Right there and then I knew that something was wrong. For Len to trace me all the way up in Maine, something had to be serious and urgent. "Cut down your vacation and come back home because I need to terminate you and myself. We are shutting down the company." I was speechless. Alice was waiting to hear what the phone call was all about. I broke the news to her as gently as I could, without creating anxieties.

MARCH 26, 1970

A date Alice and I will cherish forever. Highly meaningful for both of us. Immeasurably significant. We had waited eleven years for this day. The day Alice and I were sworn in and took the oath to become American citizens.

We needed two witnesses to testify on our behalf. I had selected Leonard Isaacson and Marvin Mann, my leading agent, to represent us. All four of us went to the Bergen County Court House in Hackensack, New Jersey and attended the ceremony. When it was all over and I had the citizenship certificates in my hand, I invited Len and Marv to a nearby restaurant. Following a few congratulatory drinks and reminiscing the tough days we had gone through, I asked Len if he would be kind enough to drive Alice home, because I had a task to perform.

I drove straight to the New York County Court building in downtown Manhattan.

I was going to see Judge Goldberg and flash my citizenship certificates in his face. This was the judge who had authorized our deportation on three separate occasions.

I had memorized a few unkind words for him, for the hardship he had inflicted upon Alice and me with his harsh decisions. As I was heading towards his chamber, I realized that they had changed the configuration of offices on the floor. I couldn't locate his chamber.

In that state of confusion, I was approached by a gentleman who asked me if he could help. I told him that I was trying to locate judge Goldberg's chamber. He asked me why was I looking for judge Goldberg. In a rather terse manner I told him that it was none of his business. "Calm down," he said "All I'm trying to do is see if I can be of help." "Well" I responded, "point me to the direction of his chamber." There was a moment of silence. "Judge Goldberg is dead," he said. He went on to say that he had died two years ago. I was stunned, as well as embarrassed. I turned to the gentleman and apologized for my rude behavior. I thanked him for volunteering to help me out. I told him that there was nothing more for me to do in the court house and wished him a pleasant day.

As I was heading towards the exit, I started talking to myself. I told myself that this was the first day of the rest of my life as an American citizen. I told myself that there was no room for revenge or negative thoughts. I reminded myself how hard Alice and I had fought for this day. Well, finally here it was. Why not enjoy it, today, tomorrow and for the rest of our lives.

It was a bright sunny day. As I was descending the steps of the court house, I literally danced every step down. It was an exhilarating experience, holding those certificates in my hands and feeling different. It was the beginning of a new life.

JOHN HANCOCK MUTUAL LIFE INSURANCE COMPANY

The termination with Lincoln National of New York came in August of 1975. I must admit that I felt a bit bitter and let down. After all, I had a very successful track record and I felt a victim in a power play between The New York State Insurance Commissioner and a board of directors in Ft. Wayne, Indiana. As silly as it may sound, those were the facts. I had to reach a decision as to my future career, not only for my sake and that of my family's, but for those agents who stuck with me and were waiting to follow me in my next venture.

Len Isaacson had joined the United States Life Insurance Company as a Vice President. He offered me a position as a General Agent but I wasn't comfortable with their system and with their compensation for the agents. I thanked him for his concern, but I turned his offer down.

Paul H. Kreuzer was the Field Vice President for the Eastern Region of John Hancock. His boss was John C. Scully, Senior Vice President in charge of General Agencies. Jack had alerted Paul about Lincoln's closed agencies. All 32 were in his region. By the time Paul approached me it was already the end of September. I liked what he had to offer and he certainly liked my record. He had arranged for a personal interview with Jack Scully and myself in Boston. It appears that they were grooming me as a Co-General Agent in their Brooklyn agency where the current General Agent Bernard Gorson was about to retire in a couple of years.

Finally, on November 1, 1975 I was hired as a Co-General Agent in Brooklyn with the understanding that I would take over as sole General Agent, following Bernie's retirement. I brought the rest of my agents with me, including Andy Koinoglou.

The agency was located on Joralemon Street, inflicted with crime. We had to carry four keys in order to get into the agency. The windows were reinforced with iron bars to prevent anyone from getting in. Not a conducive atmosphere for recruiting, let alone inviting customers to come in. I made it clear to Bernie, as well as to Paul Kreuzer that I was going to move the agency to Manhattan. The problem was the rent. I had to find a desirable building with a reasonable rent, so that our expenses would not go through the roof. Finally, after a year and a half of looking and negotiating, we rented 5,000 square feet of space at 575 Lexington Avenue, the southeast corner of 52nd Street. Excellent location. The northeastern corner of 52nd Street was occupied by the Citi Bank building, the white tower with the slanted roof.

In the spring of 1978 Bernie retired, following a very nice reception arranged for him in Boston. Paul Kreuzer had made the arrangements for Bernie and his wife Ruth to fly to Boston. Jack Scully recognized Bernie's past contributions and his loyal and faithful service to John Hancock. It was an elegant affair. Bernie had elected to stay in the agency as a personal producer in charge of advanced underwriting. I had developed a Pension and Profit Sharing Division in the agency and placed Bernie as the head of that department.

New agents who felt they had a pension case would bring in Bernie and they would share the commissions when the case was successfully concluded. Bernie would service the case thereafter annually. In addition, I had cultivated a number of accountants who would refer their pension cases to us, knowing that they would be serviced annually by a competent and knowledgeable person.

In December of 1980, Paul Kreuzer placed my name as a candidate to become Field Vice President of the Southeast Region. I had absolutely no idea. When my candidacy was approved by Jack Scully, Paul broke the news to me. I was surprised and at the same time elated. The Southeast region covered all the General Agencies from Norfolk, Virginia all the way south to Miami, Florida. The headquarters were in Atlanta, Georgia, which meant that Alice and I had to relocate. The kids were already in college. Maria was attending Columbia University and Dean was attending New York University. They were both boarding students, although they were visiting home once a while over the weekends. Alice had completed her masters degree in math at Montclair State College and she was about to become a Professor of Mathematics.

So, on January 1, 1981 I was appointed Field Vice President of the Southeast region and relocated to Atlanta. Alice couldn't join me immediately because she was teaching math at Bergen Community College and she wanted to see her class graduate before leaving the college. The very first thing I did was to travel and visit every General Agency in the region and come to know personally every General Agent. I was very fortunate to have an extremely competent Director of Agencies in the region by the name of Robert W. Canfield, Jr., CLU. Bob was a southern gentleman from Memphis, Tennessee. He was married to Sue Ellen and they had two children. Bob was a husband, a father, a recruiter for the Air Force Academy in Colorado, a referee officiating high school football games, a director of agencies, and above all a delightful colleague. Where on earth he found the time to do all these chores is beyond me. I simply accepted my good fortune to have him as a friend.

The region was doing quite well, surpassing production records year after year, which meant that our General Agents were making money. The secret to vertical growth is to have more agents. I placed a great deal of emphasis among our General Agents to keep on recruiting in order to perpetuate the growth of their agencies. Bob Canfield was quite instrumental in this effort by arranging campus recruiting in some well-known colleges in the south, like Wake Forrest, UNC, Georgia State, Georgia Tech, etc. Although we were competing with companies like Xerox, Avis, First Union, Merrill Lynch and the like, we had our share of good recruits.

Meantime Alice had joined me the summer of 1981 and we bought a house in Dunwoody, Georgia, a suburb north of Atlanta. We had two houses in New Jersey. Our winter home was in Washington Township and our summer home was south on Long Beach Island. Our town was called Surf City. We placed both houses for sale and they sold almost immediately.

In 1984 Jack Scully was promoted to become President of Retail. Retail encompassed the two marketing arms of John Hancock: the General Agencies and the Managerial Agencies. The General Agency Department had approximately 60 General Agencies under its jurisdiction, while the Managerial Department was managing about 270 Managerial Agencies across the country. The head of the Managerial Department was Senior Vice President William

Rhodes. Bill was truly a fine gentleman and he had an assistant Vice President Pete Carbone.

In 1984 Jack Scully engaged himself in an experiment. He asked me to switch places with the Field Vice President of the Southeast Division of the Managerial Department John White. John would take over the General Agencies, while I would take over the Managerial Agencies. The territories were the same and we didn't have to relocate. John was operating from Fairfax, Virginia and I stayed in Atlanta, Georgia. The idea behind this project was to unify the field forces and have them operate almost like an independent General Agent. The Managerial Department had a major problem. They were unionized. On top of that, they were not operating profitably. Jack Scully had told me, confidentially, that he expected me to convert some of the Managers into entrepreneurial businessmen. I felt I had my hands full.

During these changes, I had lost the services of my good friend Bob Canfield. He was promoted and transferred to Boston to join the Mutual Funds Department.

I now had two new Directors of Agencies. Neither one of them measured up to Bob Canfield's abilities and skills. The first thing I did again was to travel across my region and meet the Managers in person, relating my philosophy of vertical growth through aggressive recruiting which would result in financial growth. There were a number of managers who had not recruited for years. One of them was Chuck Noto, the Hollywood Agency Manager. Chuck was a bright young man who impressed me with his forward-looking attitude. When I questioned him why he was not recruiting, he told me that he had no debit to assign to the new recruit. "I'm between the ocean and the alligators," was his statement, meaning he had no more territory assigned to him. I told him that his territory was the entire state of Florida. He smiled at me. I told him that I realized my lack of knowledge in this new Managerial System, but I promised him that I would be back with a solution to his problem.

In my next visit to the Home Office, I visited with the chief administrator of debits and told him that I wanted to assign my son Dean to the Hollywood Agency under the tutorship of Chuck Noto. I told him that I didn't want my son to have a debit because he was to solicit business strictly on a referral basis across the state. I had enough connections in the state of Florida that I could refer them to my son for business. Needless to mention, the whole notion was false. Neither was Dean about to join John Hancock, nor did I have that many connections in Florida. I was simply testing the system and the administrator's firmness to the system. "No problem," was his reply. "We'll assign him an 'E' debit." "What's an 'E' debit?" I asked. I was shocked by the answer.

I was told that it was a temporary empty debit which would be replaced sometime in the future by the vacancy of an existing debit, due to death, termination or transfer of the agent occupying that debit. I already had the solution to Chuck's problem. When I returned back to the region, I visited with Chuck and explained to him the 'E' debit. "How many new agents can you recruit?" I asked. "Two or three," he said. "Make it five or ten," I said.

The next thing I did was to invite to a luncheon the union representative in my region who was an agent in the Tampa agency. His name was Bill McLain. He was disliked throughout the region. I found him to be personable and a decent human being. I told Bill that I had never managed a unionized field force. I told him that I was his boss and the teacher. He had a lot to learn from me. But when it came to union issues, he was the teacher and I was the student. I told him that I would rely heavily on his guidance. I also promised him that every time I was about to issue a memo throughout the region relating to union issues, I would check out first with him before the memo was signed. He was pleasantly surprised with my approach. He openly admitted that no officer of the company had ever approached him in that manner. I knew that I now had a friend whose advice I could rely upon.

During my first year, it was truly a challenge to change the thinking of most of the managers who were trained and ordained under the strict rules of the system. Do not violate union rules. Do not make waves. Keep the boat floating. Well, we did violate some union rules under the guidance of Bill McLain. We did make some waves, because the Home Office was now complaining about the excessive number of E debits in the region. No other region had E debits. And I was not interested in just keeping the boat floating; I wanted to increase its speed to that of a PT boat. To accomplish all these, I felt I needed to communicate directly with the agents, rather than relying on the managers to convey the message.

I started a weekly publication which was distributed throughout the region every Monday morning. It was called "Honorable Mention." I recognized every week the sales achievements of every agent in the region. I set high standards. Every agent who sold $2,500 of premium per week, his name would appear on the "Honorable Mention" and I would have something personal to write about that agent. There were several agents in the region who did not produce $2,500 of premium per month, let alone per week. All of a sudden that dormant attitude changed. Everybody wanted to see his name in the "Honorable Mention". As a result, production skyrocketed and everybody was making money. The weekly leader's production was usually in five figures. Soon the "Honorable Mention" went from a single-page newsletter to a three-to-four page publication. I was paying the price for this success. I was typing the "Honorable Mention" every Saturday morning. It used to take me anywhere from three to five hours of composing, typing and proofreading.

In 1986 Jack Scully called me to tell me that he had placed my nomination for the presidency of our subsidiary in Indonesia. Derek Sanderson was the Senior Vice President in charge of our Overseas Operations. He had arranged for an interview with me and him. It appears that John Hancock was going into partnership with the Indonesian government to open a life insurance company owned initially 70% by John Hancock and 30% by the Indonesian government. In the course of the next ten years the ownership would revert gradually to 70% Indonesian ownership and 30% John Hancock. In addition, the new president would groom a local official to become the president of the Indonesian company on the tenth anniversary.

Jack felt that with my diversified background, born in a Muslim country and understanding part of their traditions, coupled with my success in starting scratch operations, I was uniquely qualified for the position. Frankly, I didn't care for the position. Alice and I had struggled for eleven years to become American citizens.

Now that we were enjoying the fruits of our struggle, we were not about to replace living in Atlanta, Georgia with leaving in Jakarta, Indonesia.

However, out of respect to Jack for considering me and truthfully, I felt honored for being considered for the top spot in our subsidiary, I agreed to meet with Derek. We had set up a breakfast appointment in a nearby hotel. Derek started presenting me with the benefits of the position. $70,000.00 salary absolutely tax free, which considering the standard of living in Jakarta would be equivalent to $150,000.00 in the States. A chauffer-driven American car. A gardener. Two first-class trips to the States every year. Free schooling for the children. I told Derek that it sounded quite attractive for someone else but not for me. I explained to Derek that in Turkey we had a live-in maid. In our summer home on Prince Island we had a gardener attending to the landscaping of our villa. I used to drive an American car in Istanbul. And our children had already graduated from college. So all the fringe benefits amounted to a big naught. At least for me. For someone else, it was a different case.

I guess to motivate me to accept the position, Derek read me some statistics about Indonesia, the most profound being that only 3% of Indonesians owned some form of life insurance. "Can you imagine the potential when you have 97% of the population without any life insurance?" he asked me. To which I replied: "97% of the population walk barefoot because they cannot afford to buy a pair of shoes, even sandals. Can you imagine how destitute our prospects will be?" Incidentally, I told Derek, confidentially, that on the tenth anniversary John Hancock would get the boot and be thrown out. We would be lucky if we could leave Jakarta with our shirts on.

I called Jack Scully and told him that I had politely turned down the offer and once again I thanked him for the consideration.

The following year he called me back to tell me that we were opening a subsidiary in Kuala Lumpur, Malaysia and that the president's job was mine if I wanted it. Even though, he stated, Derek Sanderson didn't think that I would be interested in.

I asked Jack if the terms were the same or similar to that of Jakarta. He said they were almost identical. Once again, I thanked Jack for his consideration and told him that Derek was right in his prediction. I would not be interested in the offer.

At this point, however, I felt an obligation towards Jack to share with him what I had told Derek about the future of our subsidiary in Jakarta. Inasmuch as it was speculation on my part, and I certainly didn't have a magic ball to predict the future, I told Jack that I wished John Hancock would not engage in more partnerships in that part of the world. The final outcome would not be profitable.

Indeed, the final outcome was anything but profitable. John Hancock is no longer in Jakarta nor in Kuala Lumpur and they have not made a penny.

SUNBELT REGION

In 1989 my then-immediate boss James R. Nentwig called me to let me know that the Managerial Department was contemplating assigning a few more agencies from the southwest into my region. In addition, the Field Vice President of the Western Region was about to retire and they were contemplating including some of the western states into my region as well. If all these mergers were to take place, then I would have to move the regional headquarters to Florida.

Frankly, I couldn't see the wisdom behind the move. The Atlanta airport was one of the major airports in the country. I could fly anywhere directly without having to change planes. I told this to Jim, but it seems that he had gotten his instructions from his new boss David D'Alessandro.

Finally, the merger took place and my region was now named the Sunbelt Region, covering the southeast, the southwest and the west up to San Francisco, California.

In moving the regional headquarters to Florida, I selected Boca Raton because it happened to be between the Palm Beach airport and the Ft. Lauderdale airport. Now, I had access to two airports for my itineraries, and, even better, Palm Beach airport had a direct flight to Boston, thanks to Senator Ted Kennedy.

During the move, I lost one of my most valuable colleagues, my secretary Beatrice Lawler. Bea was an exceptional person. She was a fine southern lady with impeccable manners. Her devotion to her duties and her loyalty to the region and to myself were beyond description. Every manager in the region adored Bea, the way she handled them over the phone and the way she responded to their requests. She had developed a unique relationship with all the Office Managers of every agency in the region. Everybody loved Bea. Unfortunately, she could not come with us to Boca Raton because her mother-in-law was ailing in health and her husband Larry was the one who was taking care of her.

The Sunbelt Region covered a humongous territory, almost half of the United States. If you were to draw a line from Norfolk, Virginia across to San Francisco, California, the bottom portion represented the Sunbelt Region. As a result, I was on the road almost every week visiting the agencies. I paid particular attention to the newly acquired ones, as I was eager to introduce our philosophy, our production and ethical standards and our vertical growth system. I also wanted to establish a direct rapport with the agents through the "Honorable Mention." I wanted them to become participants as the rest of the agents in the region did.

The Sunbelt region did very well from its inception. It was hard work and extensive traveling but the results were rewarding. We came in number 1 in 1990, 1991, 1992 and 1993. We had won four President's trophies. I now had a third Director of Agencies whom I had inherited from the Western region. He was an Englishman from Leeds, Yorkshire. He helped me a lot by covering the western agencies.

METROPOLITAN LIFE INSURANCE COMPANY

Met Life was the second largest life insurance company in the country, following Prudential. One of their largest agencies was the Tampa agency in Florida, headed by Manager Rick Urso. Rick used to train his agents to sell life insurance to nurses, not only in the state of Florida, but across the country, pretending that they were retirement plans. Agents in the Tampa agency were allegedly instructed to call themselves "nurses specialists."

Following an extensive investigation by the Florida Insurance Commissioner Tom Gallagher, it was determined that Met Life auditors had spotted this deceptive practice as early as 1991 and had suggested that the training in the Tampa agency be altered. Unfortunately it continued. In addition, an agent from the Tampa agency had written a letter to the Met Life Chairman Harry Kamen and the President Ted Athanassiades, complaining about the deceptive practice. The letter went to the secretary, who in turn passed it on to the Southeast Regional Office. At this point, Commissioner Gallagher was threatening to revoke Met Life's license to do business in the state of Florida. Met Life volunteered to refund the premiums to some 18,000 policyholders around the country who had bought life insurance from the Tampa agency.

This scandal created panic among major life insurers who were doing business in Florida. One of them who panicked was John Hancock. I was told by confidential sources that the Home Office was looking into my region and more specifically into the St. Petersburg agency, which was the leading agency in the region. Its Manager Roger Hoyt was a dynamic leader who had been with the company for 29 years and who was leading the region with the most earnings. In fact, I was told that his earnings were a topic of resentment among top senior officers in the Home Office.

In 1993 Roger had earned $432,915.00—far greater than any Vice President's compensation in the Home Office. My previous boss Jim Nentwig had earned $250,962.00. Jim was replaced by Dick Hansen who had earned $243,101.00. Vice President Neal F. Smith, in charge of union relations was paid $214,988.00. There was no Vice President in the Home Office who even came close to Roger's earnings. So there was a great deal of validity behind the antipathy towards Roger. In fact, I had scheduled Roger to earn $600,000.00 in 1994 and he was running ahead of schedule in 1994. This created an uproar in the Home Office. I was further told that the Home Office was determined to keep Commissioner Gallagher from looking into John Hancock's practices and that they were going to accomplish that by doing their own cleaning and implementing new, sweeping changes.

Frankly, I didn't pay much attention to the rumors because there were no deceptive practices in the region. In fact, in October 1993 I issued a memo to all the managers in the region under the heading "Ethics" emphasizing the need to uphold a high degree of ethics in our daily practices and that "Quality Service" and "Customer Satisfaction" should be the first and foremost objectives of every associate in the region.

John Hancock was the official sponsor of the International Olympic Committee.

The winter Olympics were held in Lillehammer, Norway and I was invited to attend as the leading Regional Vice President. I must admit they treated me royally and I didn't suspect any adverse coming, even though the invitation to Roger Hoyt, as the leading Manager, and to Nat Markowitz and Nick Cinelli, the two leading agents in St. Petersburg, were withdrawn at the very last minute. That didn't sit well with me.

Upon my return from Norway, I was called by Dick Hansen to tell me that they had tape-recorded one of the seminars given by Nat Markowitz and Nick Cinelli and the tape contained several misrepresentations. In addition, they had a dozen complaints from policyholders who had purchased life insurance from the St. Petersburg agency. I asked Dick to send me the complaints so that I could investigate them. He promised me he would. I also asked Dick if he had personally seen and listened to the tape. He told me he had. I trusted him. I had no reason to suspect that he was lying to me.

However, my confidential sources had told me that David D'Alessandro had prepared a scheme where he was going to kill two birds with one stone. His long term-goal was the downsizing of the Managerial Department. At the beginning of 1993 the Managerial Department had 112 agencies. At the end of the year it was down to 83 agencies. He was about to close the St. Petersburg agency to keep Commissioner Gallagher off Hancock's doorstep, in the meantime he would use Commissioner Gallagher's threat in downsizing further the Managerial Department. I must admit I thought it was a far-fetched scenario. Unfortunately it turned out to be true.

It appears that a group of senior officers in the Home Office in Boston elected to engage in a "house cleaning" conspiracy in order to keep Commissioner Tom Gallagher from looking into John Hancock's sales practices. This group was headed by Senior Executive Vice President David D'Alessandro. He was heard in Copenhagen, Denmark at the President's Cabinet meeting, as well as in other conventions, making statements like: "We need to 'trim the fat' and become more 'lean and mean'." One of his co-conspirators was my immediate boss Dick Hansen.

On April 6, 1994 Dick Hansen called me ordering me to terminate Markowitz, Cinelli and Hoyt. As usual, the proper letters of termination were going to be drafted by the Home Office and sent to me for my signature and delivery. I voiced my reservations to Dick about the whole matter and told him that I would not sign the letters, since I was not part of the deliberations which took place, nor had I seen a single file of complaint, or the missing tape. He didn't take it kindly.

On April 12, 1994 I personally delivered the termination letters signed by Dick Hansen to Markowitz, Cinelli, and Hoyt. Both agents asked me to see and listen to the infamous tape which was the smoking gun for their terminations. I promised them that I would provide it to them. On my return to the region, I called Dick and asked him to provide me with the tape. He promised me he would. The next day, he called me back to tell me that the Home Office would not release the tape, but he had something better for me. The transcript of the tape. Not only it did make no sense to me, but I became awfully suspicious about all the accusations against the St. Petersburg agency.

Beginning of April, I started dictating memos to the file, documenting every conversation I had with every senior officer in the Home Office. The whole matter didn't make sense. There was something wrong. David D'Alessandro had manage to get very close to the Chairman & CEO Steve Brown. He would play golf with him and cater to every wish. This was not the case with the President & COO William L. Boyan. Bill was a distinguished gentleman who had been with the company for years and he had elevated himself to the Presidency by serving the company with honesty and integrity.

When I received the transcript of the tape from Dick Hansen, I couldn't find a single misrepresentation in the transcript. In fact, Dick used words like "incomplete" and "evasive" but not "misrepresentations." When I read the transcript to Markowitz and Cinelli in the presence of their Agency Manager Roger Hoyt and the Union Representative Bill McLain, their first reaction was "This is poppycock." They went on to state that the transcript was incomplete and had several blanks and flaws. Following the meeting, I pulled Bill McLain aside and solicited his opinion as to the contents of the transcript, namely if there were any misrepresentations. His answer was negative. He even expressed doubt as to the accuracy of the transcript. At this point I suspected if there had ever been a tape.

Following their terminations, Markowitz, Cinelli and Hoyt retained the services of attorney Elihu H. Berman from the law offices of Krug, Berman & Silverman, P.A., from Clearwater, Florida. Mr. Berman was going to ask the reversal of all three terminations on the ground of wrongful termination, otherwise he was going to file a suit against John Hancock.

KILLING THREE BIRDS WITH ONE STONE

In the ensuing month, David D'Alessandro, Dick Hansen and the rest of the officers involved in the conspiracy of "house cleaning" saw the window of opportunity for a triple play. How to kill three birds with one stone. How to replace the oldest Regional Vice President (I was 63 years old at the time), with a younger one while circumventing the Age Discrimination in Employment Act (ADEA); how to replace the highest paid Regional Vice President ($182,218.00) with one earning less while still tiptoeing over ADEA; and finally how to convey a very strong message to Commissioner Gallagher that we at John Hancock not only terminate our heavy guns during our "house cleaning" process, but we do not hesitate terminating officers of the Company as well. Therefore, no need to look into our sales practices.

In June, I was due to have the region's quarterly review with Dick Hansen in Boston. Instead of having a review, he handed me my termination papers charging me with complete disregard to my obligations as a Regional Vice President and also total abdication of my responsibility to protect the Company's interests. Mind you, these were the very same people who were honoring me for the past four years for doing an excellent job for the Company. In 1993 they paid me a bonus of $50,000.00 the highest ever paid to any Regional Vice President. They paid me tribute by inviting me to the Winter Olympics in Lillehammer, Norway. And they took agencies from the southwest and west, merging them into my region because they were so impressed with my performance. Had I agreed to sign the termination letters and become a member of their conspiracy, the situation might have been different.

How wrong was my termination and the conspiring plot? Wrong enough for the panel of judges from the NASD Arbitration to find John Hancock liable to the tune of $1,321,400.00 (Stathis, Hoyt, Markowitz & Cinelli combined) and order them to pay attorney fees, on top of the award. As condemning this award may have been for John Hancock and its conspiring officers, in essence it was a drop in the bucket for a Company that managed over $60 billion at the time.

David D'Alessandro had succeeded in killing three birds with one stone. He succeeded in his downsizing strategy; he succeeded in evading the law (ADEA); and he succeeded in keeping Commissioner Tom Gallagher from probing into the Company's sales practices. His success didn't end here. His record of successful maneuvering goes on.

THE METEORIC RISE OF DAVID F. D'ALESSANDRO

David came to John Hancock from an advertising agency that we were doing business with. He was assigned to the Group Department which at the time was losing money. His mission was to turn it around. Indeed, he did, although his solutions to the problem were short-lived. For instance, he slowed down the payment of claims and accelerated the sale of small group plans, which generated more revenue to the Department.

One of his first accomplishments in the area of advertising was to reshape our advertising program and to claim the Boston Marathon as the sole sponsor. There were no financial awards, in those days, paid to the winners of the Boston Marathon and the finish line of the race used to be the Prudential building. He managed to change all that. The finish line now was the Hancock Tower. And the financial awards attracted runners from all over the world, especially Africa.

The year of 1988 was an election year. David had asked for a leave of absence from the Company in order to work in Governor Dukakis' campaign. Allegedly, he was a great fund raiser among influential people. Some people heard him say that had Governor Dukakis been elected President of the United States, he would have been appointed Secretary of State. Personally, I doubt it. David had neither the personality nor the savvy to deal with Ministers of Foreign Affairs, especially with those from central European countries. But, one never knows. Money talks.

Upon his return to the Company, he was promoted to Executive Vice President and assigned to the Retail Sector to replace Herb Gold who was the outgoing Executive Vice President. His mission was to turn around the Managerial Department from a losing entity to a profitable operation. His strategy was to downsize the Department by terminating as many agencies as possible and retain only those which were operating profitably. His reward was a promotion to Senior Executive Vice President with a higher pay. In 1993 David was paid $788,052.00.

At the same time, he became very close to the Chairman & CEO Steve Brown. They were socializing and playing golf together. His relationship was not the same with the President & COO Bill Boyan who was the only stumbling block to David's assuming the presidency of the Company. Soon Bill Boyan elected to retire. His retirement, many claim, was partly induced by efforts from Chairman Brown and David himself.

David now was elevated to President & COO of John Hancock. His meteoric rise to the presidency of the Company, for an outsider, was unprecedented. There were senior officers in the Company with 20 and 30 years of loyal service who were not even considered. The speed of his rise to the top portrayed the dynamics of his strategies, maneuverability, and plain old street smarts. And the best was yet to come. Some brilliant moves on his part would record greater accomplishments in the years ahead.

John Hancock was a mutual company owned by its policyholders. As such, there were no shares to trade or buy, unless it became a stock company. One of David's brilliant moves was to demutualize the company and convert it into a stock company. This needed the majority vote of the existing policyholders. To accomplish that, David promised a number of shares of the new stock to each policyholder, the size of which depended on the type of policy they owned. Needless to mention, the vote was almost unanimous. Alice and I received several hundred shares of the new stock which opened at $17.00 a share on its first day of trading. The year was 2000. In April of 2001, *Business Week* had an article in its "Inside Wall Street" section, under the heading "John Hancock's Name Looms Large" and wrote: "Unbelievable but true: A stock that went public at 17 last year is now at 35."

This was truly one David's brilliant moves. He had many. But this one made him a multi-multi-millionaire. Every John Hancock policyholder made money under this move. But David's wealth was incomparable. Remember his compensation in 1993?

$788,052.00. In just ten years, in 2003, his compensation was $21,744,656.00. That is 27.5 times larger than what he had earned ten years ago. In fact, it created an uproar in the industry that it was excessive compensation for the Chairman, President & CEO of an insurance company. Steve Brown had already retired and David was now the sole honcho in the Company. He was Nero and Napoleon, all wrapped in one. A spokesperson defended his compensation by stating to the press that Mr. D'Alessandro's salary was only $1 million, plus $1.1 million bonus which equaled to $2.1 million. The rest was restricted stock awards and stock options.

Remember Andy Koinoglou, my associate with Lincoln National and John Hancock? In 1999, Andy sold a $1 million policy to a Greek restaurateur. Following the sale and delivery of the policy, a Merrill Lynch broker approached the restaurateur and asked him to drop the policy and instead invest the premium with him. He would end up doing better with him. Thank God, he called Andy and told him what the broker had suggested to him. Andy took the time to explain to him the benefits of the policy, what they meant for his family in the event of a premature death, and how the accumulated cash values and dividends could supplement his retirement. If he wanted to invest with the broker, he could have done that with additional funds. A year later, in 2000, the Greek restaurateur received 1,000 shares of John Hancock stock. In April of 2001, it was worth $37,000.00. And he still had his life insurance policy.

Another brilliant move on his part, which would end up accelerating his wealth by tenfold, was the sale of the John Hancock Tower and some adjoining buildings to a real estate investment firm, with the understanding that the name John Hancock would be preserved on the tower. In addition, he negotiated a long-term lease agreement, where John Hancock now was a tenant in the John Hancock Tower.

This move generated a substantial amount of cash flow into the Company. John Hancock was now a very cash-rich entity ready to be taken over. It is rumored that David himself was engaged in merger negotiations with several insurance companies, including Met Life and AIG. Of course, nobody knows, except David himself.

Finally, out of nowhere appeared this unknown Canadian insurance company by the name Manu Life which made an offer. It was approved by the stockholders and now John Hancock was a wholly-owned subsidiary of Manu Life. Incidentally, the name of the Chairman & CEO of Manu Life happened to be David D'Alessandro.

Prior to the takeover, David had amassed a large quantity of John Hancock shares, restricted, as well as options. Both shares and options ran into millions. In addition, he was entitled to cash awards, as high as 100% of his salary, according to the terms of the Compensation Committee. The Compensation Committee also allowed executive officers, above the title of senior vice presidents, to apply their cash awards in purchasing Common Stock at the prevailing price, either on the open market or through the Company. The number of shares purchased in this manner were matched by restricted stock up to 50% of the purchase.

These restricted stocks and options had a certain time period, ranging from three years to five years, before they could be exercised. However, the Compensation Committee had a provision that in the event of a *change of control* in the Company, all time periods were cancelled and all shares and options became instantly exercisable. You can appreciate, therefore, how one's wealth skyrocketed overnight.

In addition to the Compensation Committee, the Company had its Policy Committee, composed of the executive officers of the Company. The Company had adopted a mandatory stock ownership program for the members of the Policy Committee to own Common Stock in an amount equal to three times their base salary, by March 2005. In addition, the Policy Committee made a loan program available to its members. Each member could borrow up to two times his base salary. As of January 1, 2002 Mr. D'Alessandro's outstanding loan was $2,227,354.

When the Sarbanes-Oxley Act went into force on July 30, 2002 all outstanding loans were paid in full.

These were some of David's exceptional moves which made him an exceptional executive and exceptionally wealthy.

THE BRIGHT SIDE OF MY TERMINATION

How can there be a bright side to someone who loses his employment? It has been said that every letdown is followed by an uplift. There is plenty of evidence of men who were fired and ended up with better employment with higher pay. That's an uplift. One has to look for it.

In my case, the uplift was a spiritual reward. I never knew that I had so many friends who held such a high respect for me. The number of phone calls that I had received from people in the Home Office in Boston was overwhelming. So were the letters and cards. Very inspiring and encouraging. The best one came from my daughter Mary on Father's Day. I still cherish that card. It read:

"Dear Dad:

Happy Belated Father's Day. Dean told me about this weekend and I want to say, Congratulations on your new freedom.

Those contemptible pigs have shown their true colors, and it's no reflection on you. You are decent, upright, and good-hearted. You set the standards by which manhood and fatherhood are defined.

Every happiness that ever came or ever comes into my life is because I'm your daughter.

Thank you for all of it. I couldn't be more proud of you if you were Atticus Finch and Gregory Peck rolled into one. I love you. I'll see you in a few days.

Your daughter,

Mary"

And how about all the Managers in the region who got together and presented me and Alice with a nice pair of binoculars with a lovely card which read:

"Dear Jim:

We all wish you and Alice the very best in whatever the future holds for you. Whenever you do some boating—which we hope you do a lot of and use these glasses, remember those who thought a lot of you and about you.

Your Sunbelt Agency Managers"

The binoculars and the card were presented to me by Kathleen Reardon, our Manager in Anaheim, California, on behalf of all our Managers in the region, to which I responded with the enclosed letter. Subsequently, I sent her the following poem:

> So, I can safely say that I hold no regret,
> Since most of us will never forget,
> The fun we've had until I was gone,
> For those memories will be cherished for long.

And how about Ann Buckley's testimony to the NASD Arbitrators through her affidavit wherein she ranked me tops among the seven Regional Vice Presidents?

Mind you, she was a Compliance Officer and she had access to all seven regions in the Company.

More damaging to John Hancock was her determination that it was Richard Hansen who had engineered my termination and who had pressed the rest of the members of the committee for approval.

Enclosed is a copy of Ann Buckley's affidavit as it was submitted to the NASD Arbitration.

Once again, I am thankful to all those who supported me with their kind words and encouragement. May God bless you all. I will cherish those memories forever.

August 1, 1994

Ms. Kathleen M. Reardon
Agency Manager
John Hancock Financial Services
P. O. Box 4200-P
Anaheim, CA 91503

Dear Kathy:

First let me thank you for that lovely gift of a magnificent pair of binoculars. I am very appreciative of your thoughtful expression. Alice and I will put the binoculars into good use when we do some boating at Lake Lanier, Georgia, and we will fondly remember all of you.

Ron Schenk picked an exquisite card. The final paragraph reads: "It's just like you, to dream…to dare…to do." Someday, all of us may look back and take a great deal of pride for having been a member of the Sunbelt Region. For we had the vision to dream…the guts to dare…and the ability to do it.

As I have stated in my farewell message, the Sunbelt Region could not have won three Presidential Citations and two President's Trophies consecutively, had it not been for your competitive spirits and winning attitudes. It has been truly a pleasure and a privilege for me to work with you.

Alice joins me in wishing you and Paul good health and prosperity in the years ahead. Once again, many thanks for your thoughtfulness.

Fondly,

James C, Stathis, CFP
Regional Vice President

NASD ARBITRATION

JAMES C. STATHIS,
ROGER M. HOYT,
NATHAN MARKOWITZ,
and NICHOLAS T. CINELLI,

Claimants,

v.

JOHN HANCOCK MUTUAL LIFE
INSURANCE COMPANY

Respondent.

---/

AFFIDAVIT

STATE OF _____
COUNTY OF _____

PERSONALLY APPEARED ANN BUCKLEY who being duly sworn

Deposes and say:

1. In 1993 and 1994 I was Compliance Officer for John Hancock Distributors, Inc., Boston, Massachusetts. Before that I was employed in the NASD For about three years, in the Special Investigations Unit. I have a law degree from New England School of Law, although I am not a practicing attorney.

2. While employed at John Hancock Distributors, Inc., I came to know and respect James Stathis, Regional Vice President. I enjoyed working with him, and valued our professional association very highly. I ranked Mr. Stathis tops among the seven Regional Vice Presidents that I had worked with in the managerial Department. He was one I could truly trust.

3. When I heard that Mr. Stathis has been fired, I was shocked. I had not been consulted, nor had I heard anything to indicate that he might be fired. I knew they were looking into the Hoyt agency in St. Petersburg.

4. I "raised a stink" with Bob Watts (President of John Hancock Distributors, Inc., and Chairman of the Compliance Review Group). I pressed him for an answer as to why Mr. Stathis has been fired. He assured me that it was not a compliance matter and "there were other issues", and he begged me not to press him for explanations.

5. I determined that it was Richard Hansen who had engineered Stathis' termination and who had pressed the rest of the members of the committee for approval.

6. Some time after that I resigned from Hancock and accepted an offer as Assistant Vice President with The Colony Group in Boston. At the present time, however, I am at home, pregnant, expecting to give birth on or about June 26, 1996.

I give this Affidavit in the event I will be unable to attend the Arbitration hearing, and in the event that my testimony cannot be delivered by telephone.

DATED at _____ this _____ day of May, 1996.

FURTHER AFFIANT SAYETH NAUGHT.

_____
Ann Buckley

SUBSCRIBED AND SWORN TO before me this _____ day of May, 1996.

_____
Notary Public

My Commission Expires:

LANCE ARMSTRONG

A GREAT ATHLETE EMERGING FROM THE LAST MILLENIUM INTO THE NEW MILLENIUM WITH UNPRECEDENTED RECORDS OF PERFORMANCE.

Lance Armstrong has just won the Tour de France for the seventh consecutive year with record timing at the age of 33. His Herculean effort and accomplishment place him among the best athletes of the world, if not the very best athlete on earth.

For the benefit of my readers, the Tour de France is an annual event which brings in professional and amateur cyclists from all over the world to ride 2,232.7 miles across France and its mountains during the course of three weeks—23 days to be exact. Can you imagine what kind of discipline, endurance, stamina and strength it takes for a cyclist to ride 2,232.7 miles, rain or shine, for 23 consecutive days?

This sport, for years, had been dominated by cyclists from France, Germany, Italy, Belgium, Spain, and other central European and Scandinavian countries. All of a sudden, in 1999, here comes this 26-year-old American to compete among the world's best cyclists. No one gave him a chance, except himself and his coach. It would have been a miracle if he had finished among the top twenty cyclists, let alone winning the Tour. Which he did, in a spectacular fashion. President Clinton was the occupant of the White House at the time.

But there is something far more spectacular and amazing which took place prior to 1999. In 1996 Lance Armstrong was diagnosed with cancer. With extensive and sustained treatment, and a great deal of determination to overcome this dreadful disease, in less than three years he was training to enter the Tour de France. And indeed, he did. In 1999 he won his first Tour de France to the amazement of millions, except himself and his coach. The rest is history.

Let us examine the records of this history. In 2000, he entered again and to the amazement of many, he won the Tour for the second consecutive time. Many wanted to know what was he on. Lance was drug-tested hundreds of times, in and out of competition, and he was never found positive. "What am I on? I'm on a bike busting my ass for six hours a day," was his answer. In 2001, he entered again and won again for the third consecutive year. At this point, he had earned the respect and admiration of many cyclists, if not all cyclists competing against him. In 2002 and 2003, he was heavily favored and as usual he finished triumphantly first. In fact, in 2003 he set a new speed record of 25.44 miles per hour.

Many, at this point, wanted to find out the secret to his spectacular and consistent success. Lance insisted that he simply trained, worked and prepared harder than anyone else. His focus, discipline and determination were some of the key factors which contributed to his success.

2004 was a critical year. Had he decided to enter and won the Tour for the sixth consecutive time, that would have set an unprecedented record. No cyclist in the Tour's history had ever won the Tour de France for six consecutive times. Frenchmen Jacques Anquetil and Bernard Hinault, along with Belgian Eddy Merckx and Spaniard Miguel Indurain, all had won five Tours. In 2004, Lance Armstrong decided to enter and as expected he won the Tour for the sixth consecutive time, setting a brand-new record in the Tour's history.

In 2005, Lance decided that this was going to be his final entry and that he would retire thereafter. The stakes were high. The competition was keen. And his age had advanced by seven years, since his first entry. As usual, he trained hard and prepared himself better than anyone else. His final ride to victory which consisted of 89.8 miles to the 21st stage into Paris, was not without incident. It was a rainy day. The wet weather made the road slippery. Three of his teammates slipped and crashed. Lance, riding just behind them, braked and skidded but did not fall, putting his right foot to the road to steady himself. He pedaled himself up to Champs-Elysees stage to claim his crown as the grand winner of the Tour de France, for the seventh consecutive time.

"This year's Tour de France is expected to go down in the record books as the fastest ever," said Tour Director Jean-Marie Leblanc. This year's average speed over the three weeks was 25.91 miles per hour. It broke the record of 25.44 miles per hour set in 2003 when Armstrong won his fifth consecutive Tour.

Here is the finishing order of the top twelve cyclists and their timing:

1.	Lance Armstrong	86 hrs.	15:02	USA
2.	Ivan Basso	87 hrs.	4:40	ITA
3.	Jan Ulrich		6:21	GER
4.	Francisco Mancebo		9:59	ESP
5.	Alexander Vinokourov		11:01	KAZ
6.	Levi Leipheimer		11:21	USA
7.	Michael Rasmussen		11:33	DNK
8.	Cadel Evans		11:55	AUS
9.	Floyd Landis		12:44	USA
10.	Oscar Pereiro		16:04	ESP
11.	Christophe Moreau		16:26	FRA
12.	Yaroslav Popovych		19:02	UKR

John Kerry, the Democratic Senator from Massachusetts, had this to say: "What's made him so special at the Tour de France, and as an athlete, is the level of focus, discipline, intelligence, strategic ability, and obviously, his endurance—his ability to just take it on and go. Those qualities would serve Armstrong well in politics. I think he'd be awesome, he'd be a force. I just hope it's for the right party," said Kerry, an avid cyclist and longtime fan of the Tour de France.

Lance Armstrong was the perfect student of what General Resit Ertegun was teaching us. Although they lived in different times, the General's teachings and Lance's execution was flawless and with absolute precision.

Focus, discipline, determination and endurance were certainly some of the key elements in Lance's planning. His strategy to attack the mountainous roads with vigor and a lighter bike, while his competitors were gasping for air, paid off handsomely. His vision of winning the Tour and standing on the victor's stage with the yellow jersey, the famed "maillot jaune," were part of his visionary goals. The General used to call it "Visualizing The Future." The General would have been so proud of Lance Armstrong. He personified all of his teachings.

On the winner's podium set against the backdrop of the Arc de Triomphe, Lance Armstrong held his yellow cap over his heart as the American anthem was played. His three children joined him on the podium. His twin daughters, Grace and Isabelle, wore yellow dresses, symbolizing the color of the leader's jersey. His final words from the podium were: "Vive le Tour forever."

When Lance Armstrong embarks on a political career, he undoubtedly will become a great leader. Maybe, to begin with, the Governorship in Texas. At any rate, we wish him the best of success in his new career.

JAMES C. STATHIS
ROGER M. HOYT
NATHAN MARKOWITZ
NICHOLAS CINELLI

Claimants

vs.

JOHN HANCOCK MUTUAL
LIFE INSURANCE COMPANY

Respondent

Following my termination at John Hancock, I had several consultations with my son Dean as to the options available to me to file a lawsuit against John Hancock either for wrongful termination, or age discrimination, or slander, or institutional conspiracy which was the main cause, camouflaged under the notion of "failure to follow instructions." After evaluating all my options it was decided that I join Roger Hoyt, Nathan Markowitz and Nick Cinelli in one combined lawsuit. Afterall, I might add additional weight on the case with the evidence I was ready to submit.

When I visited with Elihu H. Berman, Esq., from the law firm Krug, Berman & Silverman, P.A., from Clearwater, Florida, Mr. Berman was more than willing to take over the case when he saw the evidence I had brought with me, namely the dictated Memos To The File and other pertinent documents.

John Hancock on the other hand had retained the services of the law firm Hill, Ward & Henderson from Tampa, Florida. Dennis P. Waggoner, Esq., was the designated counsel to represent John Hancock at the NASD Arbitration case.

The hearing began on June 17, 1996 in Tampa, Florida and lasted for five days. A total of eleven sessions. A panel of three Arbitrators consisting of Floyd A. Hillstrom, Esq., Robert P. Schwartz and Andrew Bolnick heard the controversy between the two parties and their respective witnesses. From the very beginning, it became obvious that the infamous tape was the smoking gun which triggered the termination of Markowitz and Cinelli. The Chief Arbitrator Mr. Hillstrom ordered Mr. Waggoner to submit the tape for their perusal. He gave Mr. Waggoner 24 hours to submit the tape. On the morning of the third day, Mr. Waggoner stated rather apologetically that he could not produce the tape. When asked why not, he stated that Boston, meaning the Home Office, could not locate the tape.

At that point it became crystal clear that there had never been a tape. During my testimony, I told the panel of arbitrators that had I known then what I knew now, I would have never signed the termination letters for Markowitz and Cinelli.

The conspiracy of the tape was further proven by counsel Ron A. Hobgood, assistant to Mr. Berman, when he asked Dick Hansen on the witness stand, if he had ever seen or listened to the tape. With his head down, he admitted that he had never seen nor had ever listened to the tape. Yet, Mr. Hobgood produced my Memo to the File wherein I specifically asked Dick Hansen if he had seen or listened to the tape. His answer was in the affirmative. It was crystal clear now that he was lying to me at the time.

When it came to Roger Hoyt's termination, Mr. Hobgood asked Dick Hansen if he recalled the morning when he called me authorizing me to terminate Roger Hoyt. After answering in the affirmative, Mr. Hobgood produced a letter signed by Dick Hansen, the very same day, addressed to Mr. Berman stating that his client Roger Hoyt was going to be given every consideration. "Which one is true? Your call to Mr. Stathis or your letter to Mr. Berman?" asked Ron. With his head down, he whispered: "I do not recall."

During his entire testimony, not once did Dick Hansen raised his head to look me straight in the face. He never looked at Roger, Nat or Nick either. He was embarrassed and humiliated, and even when he was excused by the Chief Arbitrator to leave, he walked out of the room with his head hanging down. The damage of his testimony was irreparable. He had confirmed that he was a member of the conspiracy.

On August 2, 1996 Mr. Berman was notified by the NASD Arbitration that John Hancock was found liable and that the arbitrators had decided on an award to be entered to the tune of $325,800.00 to Stathis; $775,000.00 to Hoyt; $110,200.00 to Markowitz; $110,400.00 to Cinelli. In addition, John Hancock would pay Claimants' attorney fees. Our requests for punitive damages and interest were denied.

Following the announcement of the awards, I started receiving phone calls from the Home Office in Boston, people that I had associated with all these years, congratulating me on the outcome of the arbitration. I must admit, I was overwhelmed with their consideration and thoughtfulness. Equally, I was concerned about their security, if these conversations were taped or overheard by others. One of them told me: "I don't care. I wish they would listen into this conversation. They may learn something about people."

OIL

This morning I woke up to the news that King Fahd of Saudi Arabia had died and the price of oil had gone up to a record high of $62.30 per barrel. It was repeated on almost all of the networks that the death of the Monarch would have no impact on the price of oil. True, the death in itself should have no impact on the price of oil, but the high price has a significant impact on the constant demand of high revenues sought by the Saudi Arabian kingdom.

Let me assure my readers that this is not the last of the high marks in the price of oil. We shall see much higher prices than $62.30 in the future, especially when China and India step up the speed of their economic growth. Currently, we find them in their embryonic stages of growth, yet they are devouring every commodity they can lay their hands upon, at any price. To give you an example of the magnitude of this consumption, China alone last year consumed almost half of the world's cement production; about 20% of the world's copper; nearly one third of the world's coal production and 90% of the world's steel.

As far as oil is concerned, the demand is growing exponentially every year. They import from whomever and wherever they can get it, at any price. China has forged alliances with oil-producing countries, such as: Indonesia, Iraq, Iran, Kazakhstan, Kuwait, Libya. Nigeria, Oman, Russia, Saudi Arabia, Sudan, Thailand, Venezuela and Yemen. And they are pursuing more sources in order to meet their future needs.

Back to the kingdom and the reasons for its need for higher revenues. Everybody believes that it is one of the richest countries in the world and they have so much money, they do not know what to do with it. That was true in the

60's and 70's when they had almost $300 million coming in from oil revenues, on a daily basis.

Let me repeat that: $300 million of income daily. And the price of oil was around $15.00 a barrel. Not $62.00 a barrel. That generates more than 400% of revenue.

Then what went wrong?

Let's go back to the founder of the kingdom, a Bedouin warrior called Ibn Saud who formed the house of the Saudis, later on called Saudi Arabia. Ibn Saud had 42 sons. King Fahd was his eleventh son. More importantly, he was the first born from his favorite wife Hassa who subsequently bore him six more. These seven boys had come to be known as the Sudeiri Seven.

Each one of them showed early signs of ambition with great promise for their future. Ibn Saud died in 1953. Prior to his death, he had appointed Fahd as the first-ever minister of education in the still backward, dirt-poor, but newly oil-producing kingdom.

In that capacity, and as interior minister of the monarchy from 1963 to 1975, Fahd is credited for converting Riyahd from a dirt-poor undeveloped vast area, into one of the western-style modern capitals of the world. He had one skyscraper after another looming over the city; he authorized modern housing for the residents of Riyahd; he established the Gulf's first university; he supervised the education for women; and he provided one of the most liberal medical programs for the citizens of Saudi Arabia. He was truly spending the $300 million daily income for the development of his country and upgrading the standard of living of every Saudi citizen.

A great portion of this expenditure went to the building of an army, navy and air force with the proper training of the respective forces. Most of it, if not all of it, came from the United States. In fact, King Fahd depended a great deal on the United States for the defense of his country. This was proven to be a fact during the Gulf War when Saddam Hussein invaded Kuwait. If the house of Saud stood on two pillars, one of them was Islam and the other…money. It was the latter that contributed to the phenomenal advancement of the country.

In 1975 when King Faisal was assassinated, his brother Khalid, the third of Ibn Saud's sons and in poor health, became the King of Saudi Arabia. Fahd was viewed as the strongman who was truly running the country. King Khalid was a reluctant monarch who cared more for his falcons and traditional Bedouin pursuits than the affairs of the country. Fahd was the man who took care of the state. He loved it and he commanded more respect and authority than his ailing brother King Khalid who died a year later.

In 1976 when Fahd bin Abdul Aziz bin Saud became the King of Saudi Arabia, he was at the heart of the extraordinary process which had transformed the kingdom from a primitive backwater, with barely a school, hospital or paved road, into a financial giant with commanding influence in the politics of the Gulf nations and the Arab world. No one was more intimately associated with the spreading affluence than King Fahd himself. He was offering money, grants and awards to every Arab nation in need. He was the undisputed king who was credited with the technological and infrastructural development of his country, including the social and cultural advances that underlay this extraordinary transformation.

King Fahd was now 54 years old and he was not immune from the pleasures the west could offer. In fact, one of his critics, another member of the Saud family who migrated to London and started writing openly about the vices of the kingdom, labeled King Fahd with three Bs: Blondes, booze and baccarat.

He was celebrated for his exploits at the gaming tables of the Cote d'Azur while indulging the pleasures of the flesh, preferably of light complexion.

Well, they say, all good things come to an end. This extravagant spending; the demands of the welfare system provided; the constant upgrading of the oil installations; the upgrading of the armed forces; and the benevolent donations to the Arab world, could not be satisfied with $300 million daily. Not even $600 million. The kingdom now needed a constant inflow in excess of $240 billion annually. That's almost quarter of a trillion dollars income. As a result, some of the medical benefits given to the citizens had to be curtailed. Some of the modern hospital expansions had to be postponed. And some of the free-flowing money to the Arab world had to be minimized. The good news to this downscaling, was the constant increase of the oil price per barrel. $62.00 per barrel and going higher, helps a long way.

How does this help the U.S. economy? It does not. It helps the U.S. oil companies which have been declaring record earnings by virtue of the ever-increasing oil price per barrel. President Bush has just signed the energy bill into law. Would it bring the gas price down? No. Would it stop the oil price from going higher? No. Would it help the U.S. oil companies? Absolutely. The bill contains a ton of incentives given to the U.S. oil companies to explore new resources. They may or may not. There is no guarantee that they will.

The bill also contains numerous perks, from a Santa Claus village up in Alaska to the everglades down in Florida, and a few museums and parks in between, which have absolutely nothing to do with the discovery of new energy. Every Senator managed to include some appropriations for his own state. Then what purpose does the unified energy bill serve? It was President Bush's way of saying "thank you" to the oil and gas companies for contributing generously to his pre-election campaign. Anyone who tells you differently, he is either a politician or a fanatic Republican. Make no mistake about it.

The energy bill makes provisions for Enhanced Oil Recovery (EOR). In August of 2004 the Department of Energy stated: "…EOR still holds considerable promise for recovering literally billions of barrels of oil that today are left behind in the nation's oil fields." The trouble is that most of the major oil companies such as ExxonMobil, ChevronTexaco, ConocoPhillips, BritishPetroleum/Amoco, and others have abandoned their own oil fields, and in some cases they have sold them for pennies to the dollar to small exploration companies, claiming that it is too costly for them to extract the remaining oil in the fields. Therefore, they have no oil fields to practice EOR, assuming that they develop the advanced technology under the provisions of the energy bill.

China, for instance, has developed the technology for EOR for one of its largest oil fields. Oil production increased by 223% since the application of EOR. This is how powerful this technology is. *Business Week Online* in its January 2005 issue wrote:

"The main expansions planned in the U.S. are by smaller independents. Tiny Fort Worth-based Cano Petroleum, Inc., (CFW-AMEX) which is squeezing more oil out of mature U.S. fields, is planning to boost its acquisition and development budget by at least 300%."

Let us hope that our major oil companies will take advantage of the incentives offered to them in the energy bill by developing the right technology to extract the hundreds of billions of barrels of oil left in our fields. It will stimulate the economy and it will certainly make us less dependent on foreign oil, thus improving our trade deficit at the same time.

THE PRINCIPALITY OF MONACO

Three years ago Alice and I spent a week in Monaco. We flew into Nice, France. We rented a car and drove all over the French Riviera, visiting some lovely towns with sunny beaches and panoramic views. We covered the whole gamut, from *St. Tropez* all the way to *San Remo*, the Italian Riviera. We had such a wonderful time that we decided to go back again this year.

Our hotel was the Marriott Resort in *Cap D'Ail* which is located on the border between France and Monaco. The day we arrived, there was a soccer game scheduled to be played in Monaco's Louis II stadium between Liverpool from England and Moscow from Russia. Our room offered a magnificent view of the *Fontvielle* bay with hundreds of white yachts lined up one next to each other. Most of them were from England. There was a Russian delegation of about 300 people staying in our hotel. There was a gay atmosphere. They were drinking and singing in pre-game celebration. The outcome of the game was Liverpool 3—Moscow 1.

The family of Grimaldi had a profound influence and control in the development of Monaco, dating all the way back to the 12th century. It is believed that the name Monaco comes from the *Portus Monoeci* the old port of Hercules quoted in Mediterranean legends. However, many believe that Monaco should be named "Haven of Calm," "Land of the Sun" and "Garden of Happiness." It is all that, plus more. One cannot help but admire the peaceful serenity of the country, the blue sea and blue sky without a cloud in sight.

In 1524 the Treaties of Burgos and Tordesillas recognized the full autonomy of this small state. Augustin Grimaldi was placed at the head of government. Originally Monaco was under the protection of Emperor Charles V. Subsequently, it came under the protection of Sardinia until 1890 when it came under the protection of France and it continues to this day. The palace was originally built by the Grimaldis. It has since been enlarged to its present scale and it was the late Monarch Prince Rainier III who made great improvements including the addition of the Napoleonic Museum. In fact, Prince Rainier III is credited with placing Monaco on the front page during his Monarchy. He attracted millions of tourists from all over the world and corporate headquarters including Aristotle Onassis and his shipping empire; his marriage to Grace Kelly and the birth of their three children, the Crown Prince Albert and the Princesses Caroline and Stephanie fascinated the world.

The Cathedral in the palace and the adjoining Oceanography Museum are two impressive structures. Alice and I enjoyed having dinner in the different restaurants lined up in the *Fontvielle* bay, all facing the huge rock supporting the palace, the Cathedral and the Oceanography Museum on the side. The Oceanography Museum is an imposing building constructed on a rock descending into the sea.

The architect was Delefortrie and it was inaugurated in 1910 during Prince Albert I's monarchy. To this day, it is still admired by many architects for its design and the way it emerges from the rock.

The famous Monte Carlo Casino did not exist about a century and a half ago. The site was undeveloped virgin land on the sleepy area of *Cote d'Azur*. In 1856, the owner of the land sold it for 22 centimes per square meter. It was Prince Florestan, then the Monarch, who decided to build a casino following the example of the great European spas such as Baden Baden and Marienbad. His son, Prince Charles III, consolidated his father's work by authorizing the construction of the casino on the rock, and the district was named Monte Carlo. Francois Blanc was the man named in charge. Under his direction the casino became one of the most famous institutions in Europe. Monte Carlo became the center of meeting places for the elegant society.

Frankly, Alice and I were not enthused with the gaming atmosphere of the Casino. From the exterior it is an attractive building with a regal façade. The interior is very impressive, richly decorated with hanging chandeliers and velvet drapery. The grand hall contains three roulette tables, lavishly spaced with leather chairs for the patrons. The slot machines are in a different room. The blackjack tables are in another room, and the dice table in yet another. Level of enthusiasm: Zero. Level of noise: Zero. Level of camaraderie: God forbid. After visiting Las Vegas, Reno, Lake Tahoe, Biloxi, Tunica and even the Bahamas, one wonders why on earth somebody would go to Monte Carlo to gamble. Only if he wants to be seen and rub shoulders with the elite. Most gambling places in Europe resemble funeral parlors. No enthusiasm. No fun. No talking. Long faces. Alice and I visited the Casino during our first visit three years ago. We skipped it this year. And we didn't miss a thing.

Our daily itinerary, though unplanned, turned out to be quite uniform. Breakfast in the morning at the Marriott in *Cap D'Ail,* lunch at noon in the French Riviera, depending on the town we were visiting, dinner at night back in Monaco in *Fontvieille.* If we go back again, I wouldn't change this agenda a bit.

Our favorite place in the French Riviera was *Menton.* The French call it "Pearl de la France." Indeed, it is the pearl of France. It is a lovely town, quite sophisticated, with its boutiques and restaurants lined up along the five-mile beach, including a casino. It happens to be the last town in the French Riviera before you enter Italy. In fact, as soon as you enter Italy, you can tell the drop in quality and ambience. *San Remo,* which is the first major city in the Italian Riviera, is very popular among tourists and quite cosmopolitan. Prices are slightly lower than those in the French Riviera.

Prior to *Menton,* there is another lovely town *Cap Martin.* Built on a rocky terrain, it has more of an aristocratic residence. Lovely villas and mansions built on the rock have a panoramic view of *Menton.* Most of them are secluded with elaborate gardens and palm trees, providing absolute privacy. Alice and I had a wonderful day and luncheon in a delightful restaurant built literally on a rock. We had our best swimming there. No beaches. You dive into that blue sea from the rock. What a delightful experience.

While we were vacationing in the French Riviera, unfortunately, Katrina was hitting New Orleans, Biloxi and part of Mobile. Upon our return, we were surprised to see the devastation created by Katrina on the Gulf Coast, especially the dislocation of the evacuees, not to mention the number of missing persons. As if this were not enough, four weeks later we had Rita, a category three hurricane, hitting Texas and part of Louisiana. This was the second busiest storm season on record. As of this writing, we had nineteen tropical storms, four of which developed into major hurricanes and hit U.S. coast lines. The record stands at twenty-one. The hurricane season ends November 30th. We still have two months to go. Let us pray that we will not experience the horror of another hurricane this year.

P.S.

Since writing the above, we are now faced with a monster category five hurricane Wilma, projected to land on the west coast of Florida. I call her a monster because overnight she grew from category one to category five, gusting winds in excess of 175 miles per hour. We are now one tropical storm short of matching the record of twenty-one. Here is a rundown of the tropical storms and hurricanes we have had this season:

ARLENE	Tropical Storm	Hitting Seagrove Beach, FL in June.
BRET	" "	Hitting Mexico
CINDY	" "	Hitting Louisiana, 250,000 homes without power
DENNIS	Hurricane	Hitting the Florida Panhandle on July 10th.
EMILY	"	Hitting Mexico, Yucatan Peninsula on July 18th.
FRANKLIN	Tropical Storm	Hitting Florida in late July.
GERT	" "	Hitting Mexico in late July.
HARVEY	" "	Hitting Bermuda in early August.
IRENE	Hurricane	Staying at sea in mid August.
JOSE	Tropical Storm	Hitting Mexico on August 23rd.
KATRINA	Hurricane	Hitting LA/MS/AL in late August.
OPHELIA	"	Hitting the Carolinas in mid September.

PHILIPPE	Hurricane	Hitting the Atlantic Ocean.
RITA	"	Hitting Texas & Louisiana in late September.
STAN	"	Creating mudslides in Mexico early October.
TAMMY	Tropical Storm	Heavy rain in Eastern U.S. mid October.
VINCE	" "	Heavy rain in Europe.
WILMA	Hurricane	Hitting west coast of Florida. October 24th.

The U.S. National Hurricane Center informs us that Wilma was the last name in the alphabet. The next tropical storm will be named from the Greek alphabet, starting with Alpha.

Well, tropical storm Alpha is already pounding Haiti and the Dominican Republic with winds gusting at 55 miles an hour and dumping over 6 inches of rain. It is further predicted that Wilma and Alpha may clash together as both head towards north.

Alpha has broken the record, making 2005 the busiest tropical storm season ever recorded.

ST. NICHOLAS GREEK ORTHODOX CHURCH

Wykoff, New Jersey

This is a story that needs to be told. It involves a delightful lady by the name Pauline Blum. I am sure most of you have read at some time novels "from rags to riches." Pauline's story is truly an exceptional one.

Before I start with Pauline's story, however, I need to give credit to our beloved friends Doris and Cecil Hannaford who encouraged me to write about Pauline. Doris and Cecil are longtime good friends and neighbors with whom we get together twice a week and have dinner. Following dinner, we play our favorite game called "Jokers and Pegs" which is a very entertaining game played with two decks of cards and four elaborate boards with pegs. It can also be played with six people.

The other night, following our dinner and game, we were looking at some old pictures when we came across a picture of Pauline taken together with Alice's mother in Athens, Greece. That got me started telling Doris and Cecil about Pauline's life. They were so moved, they insisted that I should include the story in my book.

When Alice and I bought our first house in Washington Township, New Jersey, we had joined a private social club with swimming pools and tennis courts. One Saturday morning we took the kids to the club when we met, for the first time, Pauline, her husband Bill and their eight kids. Instantly, we became the best of friends as if we had known each other for years. Pauline was enchanted with Alice and myself, and Bill and I started on our favorite subject "the stock market."

Bill had a very elaborate and extensive portfolio of high-grade securities which he had accumulated since childhood under the guidance of his father, who was a strict and authoritarian German. Bill never married, until he met Pauline in his late forties. His entire occupation was taking care of his investment portfolio. The annual dividend income in itself was well over six figures, for which Bill had no need. So he kept on reinvesting part of the dividends back into new securities. Mind you, we are talking 1964/1965. In those days $125,000/ $150,000 of investment income annually was a most enviable revenue. People working in executive positions, full time, were not earning that kind of money.

The story goes that Pauline as a young girl met this Greek sailor in the merchant marine who charmed her into marrying him and impregnated her with their first child. He left and came back next year, when Pauline became pregnant again. These annual visits continued for eight years, resulting in the birth of eight children when he finally disappeared.

In the meantime, Pauline's life went from bad to worse as she tried to raise eight children while working as a waitress in a nearby restaurant. Feeding them was a task in itself, buying them clothes and shoes and sending the older ones to school became a formidable task at her minimal wages and tips. In spite of her insurmountable problems, however, one thing she endured upon was her faith in taking the children to church every Sunday morning. Never missed a Sunday. She felt this was one source of inspiration for the children to learn right from wrong, to form their inner character, since there was no father at home to look up to for guidance. In her mind, the church provided the divine guidance.

Unfortunately, due to the lack of better judgment from the priest and probably some complaints from insensitive parishioners, the priest asked Pauline from now on to enter the church from the side door so that the regular parishioners would not have to see Pauline and her eight kids, sometimes well dressed and sometimes not so well dressed, parade through the main entrance. The pain was immeasurable. It hurt her so much. But it didn't stop her from taking the kids to the church every Sunday. If anything, her determination was fortified and she deeply believed that she was doing the right thing for her children.

Bill's father had passed away. Bill was now in his late forties, still a bachelor, with his only preoccupation, his investment portfolio. Every noon and night he went to the restaurant for his lunch and dinner. He kept an eye on Pauline and over time he secretly fell in love with her. Finally, one day he proposed marriage to her. Pauline was stunned. She asked what would happen to her eight children. He promised to adopt all of them and further promised to send each and every one of them to college. Pauline felt Bill was sent to her by God.

One day in the club, Bill asked me if I could or would donate $1,000.00 for a worthy cause. I said sure. I had no reservations on Bill's judgment. He was such an upright and straightforward gentleman. I said, may I ask what is it for? He said that Pauline had asked him if he would build a church for her, so that she could take her eight children and walk though the main entrance without any objection from anyone. And Bill had promised her that he would. However, he needed parishioners to support the church. He had lined up a few. He mentioned the names to me and all of them were friends or neighbors, including Dr. Kirk Kalemkeris who was our family physician and a renowned surgeon in Bergen County. At the time, all of us belonged to the church in Patterson, New Jersey. So, thirteen families with $13,000 initial capital and the balance funded mostly by Bill, went out and bought a lot in Wykoff, New Jersey and laid the initial foundation of our new church.

When we went to the Greek Archidiocese and asked the Archibishop to assign a priest to our new church, he laughed at us. He said with thirteen families? You need a minimum of a hundred families, if not more, to support a church. He declined our request.

Dr. Kalemkeris countered by telling the Archibishop that there are other Orthodox Archidioceses that would welcome us. For instance, the Syrian, the Russian, the Bulgarian and others.

We managed to hire a retired priest from New England, Father Nick Ksedias who was more than willing to go through the pains of starting a new church. In the meantime, other Greek families from Washington Township, Westwood, Ridgewood, Upper Saddle River, Wykoff and adjoining communities started joining in. Bill Blum through his banking connections was providing all the necessary mortgages. In reality, he was placing securities as a collateral.

In one of our board meetings (the thirteen families) discussing finances, Bill came up with an additional demand of $25,000.00. The question raised was if we should donate $2,000.00 each of us, or go to the bank for a long-term loan. Father Nick happened to be present in the meeting. He interrupted the discussion by asking us to do nothing for a few days because he was going to approach a connection of his.

Sure enough, Father Nick came back with a check for $50,000.00 issued by a Jewish donor who was a long time friend of Father Nick. Immediately, we formed a committee of three persons, headed by Bill Blum to go and visit this generous donor and express our gratitude. When asked if there was anything we could do for him, his answer was: "Have you named your church yet?" The answer was no. "Then," he said, "why don't you name it Saint Nicholas?" To which Bill replied: "St. Nicholas it shall be."

There is the beginning of the St. Nicholas Greek Orthodox Church in Wykoff, New Jersey, supported today by a thriving community of six hundred families. Since our initial structure, the church has been significantly enlarged with a dome. Additional lots have been bought for parking and a Sunday school has been built on the premises.

Bill and Pauline passed away after moving to Long Beach Island, south of New Jersey. So did Dr. Kirk Kalemkeris, survived by his wife and two daughters. Alice and I are among the very few survivors from the original thirteen families which built the St. Nicholas Greek Orthodox Church, thanks to the generosity of a German groom who wanted to keep his wedding promise to his Greek bride......"Build me a church."

ONE SHINY LINCOLN PENNY

I have a habit of picking up pennies from the road or wherever I find them. Once my eyes catch a penny, I bend down and pick it up. I may be dressed in my tuxedo, coming out of the Waldorf Astoria. I'll bend down and pick up the penny, or nickel or dime. It makes no difference.

Back in the late 60's, Len Isaacson, his wife Diane, Alice and I decided to fly to Reno, Nevada and have fun for a few days. We had been together to Las Vegas on many occasions, as well as to Lake Tahoe, but we had not stayed in Reno.

The second day of our arrival, we decided to get out of our hotel, the Hilton, and hit the rest of the casinos in town. We had fun. We lost in some and won in others. It was about four o'clock in the afternoon when we decided to return back to our hotel. We were about to cross an intersection when my eye caught a shiny penny resting in the middle of the intersection. The afternoon sun rays were hitting it just right, which made the penny ever so brighter and shinier. I told Len that I was going to pick up that penny. He told me that I was crazy. I was going to be killed. I was going to be rolled over not by one car but by several cars. The intersection had no traffic lights. Each section had a stop sign and the cars were alternating.

In the middle of that discussion, all of a sudden I find Len jumping in the middle of the intersection and directing traffic. I heard him shout rather loudly: "You better come and pick up this penny or I'm going to get killed here." Needless to say, I picked up the penny. It was a shiny, new mint, Lincoln penny. We all laughed on our way to the hotel about my idiosyncrasy and my peculiar habit of picking up pennies.

When we arrived at the hotel, we decided to go to the coffee shop and have a cup of coffee with dessert. In those days Keno tickets were 70 cents each. I pulled out a Keno ticket and started jotting down numbers which were our birthdays. In those days we had a dog named "Hop." I asked Alice how old was Hop. She said, "Seven."

So I jotted down the number seven also. All together I had selected seven numbers.

When I handed the ticket to the Keno girl, she asked me if I wanted a 70-cent ticket or one dollar. I told her to make it a dollar ticket.

There were several Keno boards posted all around the coffee shop. As the numbers started coming out, I noticed, to my surprise, that all seven numbers had come out.

I was shocked. I couldn't believe my eyes. I told Alice: "Poops, I think I've got it."

She gave me a strange look, picked up the ticket from my hand and she started comparing the numbers to the Keno post. "My goodness, I think you've got it," she said. By this time, Len, who has been following our surprised reactions, said: "Stop pulling my leg. Let me see that ticket." After checking the numbers, I heard him say: "Jim, you've got all seven numbers."

At this point, Diane, who had been sitting very quietly, jumps off the table, raises her two fists and puts out a loud scream. The whole coffee shop was staring at our table. We knew we had won. But we had no idea how much we had won. So I pulled out the brochure and read that seven out of seven on a dollar ticket paid $8,000.00.

The story should happily end here. But there is another story to the story.

I handed the Keno girl who had sold us the ticket a $500.00 tip. All of a sudden she burst into tears. I knew she wanted to say thank you, but she was crying so hysterically that the words couldn't come out of her mouth. Finally, after calming down, she told us that she had a car which she couldn't drive because it needed four new snow tires. Her next door neighbor who also worked at the Hilton, the morning shift starting at 6:30 AM, used to give her a lift. So she had to get up at 5:30 in the morning to get her lift, even though her shift didn't start until 2:00 o'clock in the afternoon. Now, with the $500.00 she could buy four new snow tires and sleep all the way till noon, without imposing upon her neighbor.

End of story? Not yet.

I had offered Len and Diane to share part of our winnings. Instead, they elected to have our return flight tickets upgraded to first class, which we did. After deducting 20% withholding taxes, the tip, and the upgrading, we were left with just about $5,000.00 which I handed over to Alice and asked her to do whatever she pleased with.

Alice went to the bank and bought fifty pieces of gold coins, Krugerands, at $100.00 a piece and placed them in the safety box. Time went by and gold skyrocketed to $850.00 an ounce. We sold most of the Krugerands at $800.00 a piece and still have some.

Diane summed it up nicely. She said God placed that shiny penny in the intersection, so that I could pick it up and be happy; so that the Keno girl could buy four new snow tires and be happy; and all four of us ended up having a wonderful vacation at Reno and be happy.

End of story.

EVANGELICAL NONSENSE

Last Tuesday, November 8, 2005 election day, the citizens of Dover, Pennsylvania cast their vote by ousting all eight members of their school board because they were supporting "intelligent design" as an alternate theory to evolution.

Well, this didn't sit well with the evangelical circles around the country. One of them, conservative Christian televangelist Pat Robertson decided to speak out: "I'd like to say to the good citizens of Dover if there is a disaster in your area, don't turn to God. You just rejected Him from your city." Have you ever heard of a clergyman making such a mindless statement? Absolute nonsense.

Of course, this is not the first time Pat Robertson has made such idiotic statements. In 1998, he warned the city of Orlando, Florida that it risked earthquakes, hurricanes and terrorist bombs because the city allowed organizations to put up rainbow flags in support of sexual diversity. More recently, he made headlines by calling for the assassination of Hugo Chavez, President of Venezuela, a vocal critic of President George W. Bush. In other words, Pat Robertson can call for the assassination of anyone who disagrees with his philosophy, even if that person happens to be the head of another nation. Mind you, this man is a Christian and he preaches Christianity through his televised program.

Pat Robertson is the founder of the conservative Christian Broadcasting Network and Christian Coalition. His 700 Club claims to have a daily audience of around one million. It also claims that its broadcast is translated into more than 70 languages around the world. What would the world think of such a man with such power and such faith making such brainless statements?

One commentator during a recent interview made the following statement: "Some of the evangelical preachers raise money in *dissent*, never with *consent*." So true.

I remember, years ago, the case of this southern evangelican preacher who was arrested by the police in New Orleans for picking up prostitutes for sex. Sunday morning he would get on the pulpit and tell his parishioners, in tears, that he had sinned. And money would pour in by the thousands.

The ousted eight school board members were trying to introduce "intelligent design" to high school science students as an alternative to the theory of evolution. Adherents of "intelligent design" argue that certain forms in nature are too complex to have them evolved through natural selection and must have been created by a "designer," meaning a higher power. Opponents of this absurd theory say it is the latest attempt by conservatives to introduce religion into the school science curriculum.

The Dover case sparked a trial in federal court that gained nationwide attention after the school board was sued by parents backed by the American Civil Liberties Union. The board ordered schools to read students a short statement in biology classes informing them that the theory of evolution is not established fact and that gaps exist in it. What a sneaky and devious way to poison young minds and create confusion and doubt.

A decision in the case is expected sometime this year.

Pat Robertson is a former Republican presidential candidate. Can you imagine the course our country would have taken if he had been elected president? He would have ordered the assassination of everyone who disagreed with his views, policies or philosophy. Thank God he didn't. Which proves that God is on our side.

P.S.

Today, Tuesday, December 20, 2005, a federal judge ruled that "intelligent design" cannot be mentioned in biology classes.

U. S. District Judge John E. Jones III said that the Dover Area School Board members violated the Constitution when they ordered that its biology curriculum must include the notion that life on Earth was produced by an unidentified intelligent cause. Several members repeatedly lied to cover their motives even while professing religious beliefs, he said.

"The citizens of the Dover area were poorly served by the members of the Board who voted for the ID policy," Jones wrote. "We find that the secular purposes claimed by the Board members amount to a pretext for the Board's purpose, which was to promote religion in the public school classroom," he wrote in his 139-page opinion.

Earlier this month, a federal appeals court in Georgia heard arguments over whether evolution disclaimer stickers placed in a school system's biology textbooks were unconstitutional. A federal judge in January ordered Cobb County school officials to immediately remove the stickers calling evolution a theory, not a fact.

WILL THE COLTS FINISH WITH A PERFECT SEASON 16-0?

That is the question many football fans have been asking lately. This past Sunday, the Indianapolis Colts beat the Cincinnati Bengals 45-37 extending their undefeated record to an NFL-best 10-0. This is truly an enviable record.

Since the 1972 Miami Dolphins' perfect season 14-0, only four teams have reached 11-0 and all four went to the Super Bowl, three of them winning it. Next Monday night, the Colts are playing the Pittsburg Steelers. A win will elevate them to 11-0.

That will make the Colts the fifth team to start the season 11-0 since the Miami Dolphin's perfect season 14-0 back in 1972. A truly rare milestone for the Colts.

Here are the seven teams which started their season with 10-0 and faced their first loss, ending their streak of consecutive victories:

Wins	Year & Team	First Loss	Season Outcome
10	1975 Minnesota Vikings	30-31 @ Washington	12-2 Lost NFC Divisional
10	1990 NY Giants	13-31 @ Philadelphia	13-3 Won Super Bowl

Wins	Year & Team	First Loss	Season Outcome
10	1990 SF 49'ers	17-28 vs. LA rams	14-2 Lost NFC Cham'hip
11	1984 Miami Dolphins	28-34 (OT)@ S Diego	14-2 Lost Super Bowl
11	1991 Wash Redskins	21-24 vs. Dallas	14-2 Won Super Bowl
12	1985 Chicago Bears	24-38 @ Miami	14-2 Won Super Bowl
13	1998 Denver Broncos	16-20 @ NY Giants	14-2 Won Super Bowl

Right now the Colts are the best team in the league. However, the remaining six games in the regular season become more meaningful and certainly more challenging. Can they win them all? The odds are against them. Take a look at the table above. However, I believe they can, if each and everyone of the Colts players has a deep belief that they can. They need to stay together, practice well, maintain an excellent communication and above all...believe in themselves. They need to start visualizing Super Bowl Sunday.

If I were to give one piece of advice to Coach Dungy, it would be to go out and buy 50 copies of *Think And Grow Rich* by Napoleon Hill. It was published in 1940. Since then it has had numerous reprints. It is a powerful book that stands the test of time. He should distribute it to all players and coaches and ask them to read it and read it again. They do not need the money to become rich. They all have multi-million-dollar contracts. But they do need the powerful messages conveyed by Napoleon Hill therein. The determination, unyielding determination, to win. The desire, burning desire, to finish 16-0.

The belief, deeply rooted faith that they will go all the way to the Super Bowl. And visualizing their glorious victory on Super Bowl Sunday.

Eleanor Roosevelt once said: "The future belongs to those who believe in the beauty of their dreams."

That's what the Colts need to do. Believe in themselves and believe in the beauty of their accomplishment come Super Bowl Sunday.

We'll find out if my prediction comes out to be correct.

P.S.

No. It didn't. The Colts finished the regular season 14-2 and this past Sunday, January 15, 2006 they were eliminated during the first round of the playoffs by the Pittsburg Steelers at home. Mind you, this was the very same team that beat the Steelers on a Monday night televised game, recording their eleventh consecutive victory.

Thirteen straight wins, home field advantage throughout the playoffs, a week off to rest the entire team, and the conference's No. 1 seed—all for a big naught. What went wrong? They surely lost their confidence.

Heading into the divisional round of playoffs, it was a well-recorded fact that home teams were 49-11 in this round since 1990. There was an 82% chance of road teams losing when they showed up at the home of a well-rested No. 1 or No. 2 seed. The Colts had all the odds in their favor. Plus they were facing a team which they had already beaten during the regular season.

Peyton Manning's playoff record is now 3-6 with last week's loss to the Steelers.

For all its greatness, for all its records and for all the talent, Peyton Manning could not deliver when it counted most.

If there has ever been a need to read *Think & Grow Rich* by Napoleon Hill, that need is now. The Colts and the coaches have the winter, spring and summer at their disposal to do all the reading and planning for the next season.

LIMITED PARTNERSHIPS

During the 1960's there was an abundance of tax shelters being marketed with high deductions. The riskier the partnership, the higher the deductions. Some of them were put together so loosely that they couldn't pass an IRS audit. IRS would disqualify all deductions and charge the limited partners with penalties and interest on unpaid taxes.

I had a client who was employed by United Artists. One day Max calls me and tells me that they had a picture ready to be released soon which was going to lose a lot of money. He called it a "dog." The name of the picture was *Last Tango in Paris*. It was an X-rated movie with Marlon Brando in the leading role. According to Max, our society was not ready to go and see an X-rated first class movie with a first-class actor in the leading role. It was bound to lose money. So, Max asked me if I had some high-income clients who would be interested in coming in as limited partners and absorbing the high losses.

I had a client, a physician, a plastic surgeon on Park Avenue, who was buying tax shelters to offset some of his high income. He had just been hit hard on a chinchilla-growing tax shelter which was disqualified by IRS. I felt he was the ideal candidate to invest in such a movie. So, I recommended him. From the opening week, *Last Tango in Paris* started breaking records at the box office. Instead of losses, the limited partners were hammered with steady income. After playing for several weeks in major theaters across the country, it was about to be withdrawn when Marlon Brando visited New York City and was harassed by a persistent photographer. Brando punched him on the nose and in the process he broke a bone in his fist. The very next day *The New York Post* came out with a large picture on the front page, showing Brando punching

Giallella. That did it. There was a flood of renewal showings coming in from all the theaters across the country.

The picture went on for a few more weeks, adding additional revenue to the shares of the limited partners.

It was obviously the wrong recommendation and the wrong choice of partnership. I had to make it up for my client. This time, I formed my own limited partnership, financing a tanker for another client of mine. I included a few more physicians, a restaurateur and a florist. I also had our attorneys apply to the IRS for guidance, since there was no precedent of a tanker ever being syndicated. The IRS usually does not give advance approval. However, they may offer some guidance, especially when there was no precedent. The success of my first tax shelter prompted me to proceed with a second one, this time syndicating a cargo vessel. What a disaster. I had included several physicians along with a baker. As usual, the ship was sailing under Panamanian flag, with Greek officers and a crew from Central America, mostly from Honduras and Guatemala.

On its maiden voyage, the ship was heading for St. John's in Canada to load Christmas trees for delivery to Nigeria. It was caught in a horrendous storm 200 miles off the coast of New England, battered with 18-foot waves. Being in a ballast condition, it was tossed like an empty shell in rough seas. It became disabled by suffering heavy engine damage. There were several wounded sailors, one in critical condition with a large opening in his skull. They needed immediate medical attention. I was in constant touch with the captain. He would call me every fifteen minutes, keeping me abreast of the situation.

I decided to hire a tug boat from the Boston harbor to go out to the ship and bring in the wounded to be transported to the Boston General Hospital. The tug boat company asked for $4,000.00 payable immediately before the boat sailed out. I had no choice. I authorized the payment immediately through our bank. At this point, my banker got concerned, asking why I was expediting a tug boat to the ship. What was wrong with the ship? Bankers Trust had extended us a loan holding the vessel as a collateral. Now they had a disabled ship, as a collateral, whose value had dropped drastically. I calmed my banker down and promised to keep him informed as the events unraveled. It was now late in the afternoon. Soon it was going to be dark. I was wondering how the tug boat would be able to find the ship in the middle of the stormy night.

Sure enough, three hours later I got a call from the tug boat that they couldn't find the ship and that they had returned to Boston. They also had the audacity to tell me that they would keep the $4,000.00 as fee earned for services performed. I had serious reservations in my mind if they truly made an effort to reach the ship. However, I was in no position to argue my suspicion. I had a more serious problem at hand. I had several wounded sailors who needed immediate attention.

The tension was killing me. The degree of my anxiety was indescribable.

I remembered my General's teachings. He used to tell us in case of an emergency, the worst thing you can do is to panic. Stay calm, stay focused. Concentrate on the problem, apply all your resources until the problem is resolved.

At 1:00 AM I called Senator Williams. I had never spoken with him before. I had awoken him. I apologized for disturbing him that late at night. I told him that I was in desperate need of help. I acquainted him with the entire situation and asked for his help. He asked me to stay awake. He was going to call me back in couple of hours. Sure enough, a little over than hour, he called me back to inform me that he had just authorized a C-5 transport plane to take off from North Carolina and fly over until it spotted the ship. Once the ship was spotted, it would coordinate the location with a Coast Guard Cutter which would approach the ship and transport the wounded personnel. I thanked the Senator and conveyed the message by phone to the captain of the ship who was anxiously awaiting a message of hope.

Later on, I was told by the captain that the Coast Guard Cutter could not approach the ship because of the high waves and wind. They shot a rope with a basket and the wounded were transported one at a time in the basket. They also sent them with the basket fresh water, canned food and bread. It was such a relief.

When the storm subsided, I negotiated with the Moran Company in Brooklyn to send a tug boat and bring the ship to the Brooklyn Navy Yard. It cost me $7,500.00. It took them two and a half days to bring in the ship. A truly bargain fee compared to the $4,000.00 for three hours with no results. I had a good insurance broker who facilitated the filing of all the claims. The insurance company paid all the medical bills and settled the claims filed by the wounded sailors. They denied the $4,000.00 tug boat fee but they honored the $7,500.00 fee from Moran.

How on earth I survived this trauma without getting a stroke or a heart attack is beyond me. The final blow came when Bankers Trust called for the payment of the loan. I told my banker that I was going to put up the ship for sale and that Bankers Trust was going to be the very first to be paid from the proceeds of the sale.

None of the limited partners were aware of the trauma I had gone through. I issued a memo and informed them that the ship had suffered engine damage due to the storm. It was going to be placed for sale and that the net proceeds were going to be distributed to all limited partners as final payment. In essence, they broke even. Between the losses which they took as tax deductions and the final payment, they broke even.

Following this experience, I decided that any future limited partnerships would have to deal with a more stable product than ships and movies. I decided that such a product would be real estate. Real estate offered stability, deductibility through depreciation, steady income, no unusual risks, and gradual appreciation over the years. So, I was set that my next limited partnership would be real estate, as soon as I had targeted the right building at the right price and at the right location.

My good friend and neighbor Joe Giardina and his wife Sylvia were ready to join me as partners as soon as the occasion presented itself. A real estate broker in Brooklyn by the name Louise Pfister brought to our attention a ten apartment building owned by a judge who was about to retire and willing to sell. Louise warned us that the judge was a tough person to negotiate with. Joe and I visited with the judge and after some skillful bargaining we persuaded the judge to sell the building to us for $20,000.00 down and we were to assume the existing mortgage as well as the liability of paying $250.00 quarterly to the Brooklyn Benevolent Society which owned the land.

The day of the closing, I came in with my check for $10,000.00 but Joe had forgotten to bring his checkbook. The judge was furious. He called us irresponsible, among some other adjectives.

After allowing him to let off his steam, I proposed to the judge that I would issue a check for $10,000.00 for Joe, with the understanding that the judge would not deposit it immediately, allowing me a few days to deposit the funds to cover it. That did it.

We named the partnership ALVIA Properties. After our wives' names. ALice and SylVIA. We kept the property for some 30 years with Joe managing it.

Louise was so impressed with Joe and me, that a month later she came back with another proposition, two buildings in Manhattan, one on 1st Avenue and the other adjacent on 10th Street, occupying the northeast corner of 1st Avenue and 10th Street. She was proposing a partnership of four—herself, her father, Joe and I. Each of us would invest $10,000.00 and assume the existing mortgages. We did it. A few years later, Mrs. Helmsley, just before she was indicted and served her prison term, was offering $1 million for both properties. Ultimately, Louise bought our share (Alice and I) in the partnership for quarter of a million dollars. We used IRS section 1037 and used the funds to buy another property in Atlanta.

Another dear couple of ours, Manny and Alice Ayvas who owned a beauty saloon in Emerson, New Jersey had heard the story about our partnership with Joe and Sylvia, and they expressed interest to join in whenever we formed our next limited partnership. In January of 1980 I was transferred to Atlanta, Georgia as a Regional Vice President of the Southeast Region of John Hancock. Alice couldn't join me immediately because she was teaching math at Bergen Community College. She called me from the office of a real estate broker in Yonkers, New York telling me that she was about to make a counteroffer on a ten-family residential building in Yonkers owned by a Hungarian engineer who wanted to sell and move to Florida. She had consulted with Manny and Alice and they were willing to come in as partners. Furthermore, Manny had expressed interest in managing the building since Alice was going to move to Atlanta with me. The circumstances were so ideal that I couldn't help but authorize the purchase.

Following graduation of her class at Bergen Community College, Alice submitted her resignation and in July of 1980 she moved south to Atlanta. The first thing she did was to buy a town house in a nice neighborhood in Dunwoody, Georgia. Meantime, Manny and Alice were so thrilled with their new acquisition, they told us that they wanted to participate in more partnerships. So, Alice took it upon herself to go out hunting for residential properties. Within a short period of time, she bought a ten-family and a twelve-family residential building. We named our limited partnership with Manny and Alice *Big Apple Investors.*

It appears that my decision to switch to real estate turned out to be an astute one.

Alice became a sharp negotiator in choosing and purchasing properties and a very efficient manager. Now in our retirement years, we both have something to do and the partnerships are keeping us young.

OMIROS
FROM THE STROKES OF A MASTER

Omiros is a contemporary artist, considered by many to be the master of abstract expressionism. Born in Istanbul, Turkey from Greek parents, he left in his early twenties for Paris, France to explore the limits of his talents in abstract expressionism. That's where he met his wife Rena and both became French citizens.

Subsequently, they migrated to the States and became American citizens along with their two sons, both renowned psychiatrists in New Jersey.

Alice and I have known Omiros and Rena for the past forty years. Unfortunately, Rena passed away last month after a prolonged illness. We have some lovely memories with both of them, especially when we lived in New Jersey. Prior to her retirement, Rena was employed as a translator in the United Nations. She spoke five languages fluently: English, French, Greek, Turkish and Armenian.

Omiros is an adventurer and it is illustrated in his art. He is not afraid to pursue the unknown. He is a free soul and his imagination runs on a broad scale. He draws his creative energy from all places at all times, like a river, flowing through countries and boundries following the course of history. Even when he articulates on a given subject, he poses several "whys?" probing for deeper meanings.

When we lived in New Jersey, we used to get together frequently to play bridge. Following the game, while having coffee and dessert, it was almost inevitable that we would engage in a debate on subjects ranging from Goethe,

Alexander the Great, to Ronald Reagan, the then President of the United States. We would often discover or learn something new.

In 1983, Omiros published an exceptional book of art titled *Byzantine Art, A Contemporary View*. It was a masterpiece containing some 420 color plates. The book quickly became a collector's item and treasured by art lovers. One of the paintings we bought from Omiros is included among the 420 color plates. It is an exquisite one. It portrays Jesus Christ performing the miracle in Canaa when he converted the water into wine. Aside from the striking colors, which is one of Omiros' strength, for the first time Omiros used gold along the rest of the vibrant colors. The circle of light, or halo, above Christ's head is in pure gold. So is the signature "Omiros."

Seventeen years later, in 2000, Omiros published another masterpiece titled *Omiros, Abstract and Beyond* which encompasses his abstract works from 1953 to 2000 in over 475 colorfully rich pictures. Page 353 illustrates another painting of ours we bought from Omiros titled *Four Seasons: Spring*. It is an absolute delight to look at.

The array of colors and the masterful strokes of the brush painted on silk, make the entire composition a wonder to look at. It is a large painting. It measures 26" x 35".

Omiros has given numerous exhibits in major cities all over the world. In the fall of 2000 he attended a fashion show in Paris. He was motivated by the beauty and the gracious moves of the models. As soon as he came back, his brush produced a series of fashion models portraying their wares. The beauty of each painting is indescribable. The colors are stunning. Some are in the collection of his sons Dr. Paul Hrisu and Dr. Emmanuel Hrisu. Alice and I publish a monthly magazine on the internet *www.midtowngazette.com*. If you were to click on past issues and go to issue #10, January 19, 2001 you would observe one painting folding after another. It is truly a magnificent sight.

Now that Rena is gone, Omiros has devoted his time into more painting. I do not know of any living artist that has produced more than Omiros. The galleries around the world will have a bonanza in selling his art over the years.

THE ECONOMIC STATE
OF OUR NATION

It is with a heavy heart that I write the following passages because it seems to me that nobody gives a damn, including our current administration which is totally oblivious of the tremendous economic burden they have placed on us, on our children, and on future generations. It appears that they are mentally deficient when it comes to their fiscal policies. President Bush takes the easy way out by claiming that he is not an economist. One does not have to be an economist to distinguish right from wrong. In addition, he employs several people in his administration who have had an education on economics.

Currently, we are facing a double headed dragon which is going to devour us soon with both heads. One head is our trade deficit, and the other our budget deficit. Let me share with my readers some figures which were recently released by the administration which will upset any reasonable person's tranquility.

The U.S. trade deficit soared to an all time high of $725.8 billion in 2005, due to record imports of oil, food, cars and other consumer goods. This colossal debt is on top of the $617.6 billion trade deficit in 2004. In other words, in the course of just two years we have managed to increase our trade deficit by $1.343 trillion. An astronomical debt in just two years.

America's deficit with Canada, China, Europe, Japan, OPEC, Mexico, South America and Central America has reached an all-time high. And the trend continues with more imports than exports. Where are we heading? All these nations are holding IOUs which they can decide to redeem at a moment's notice, especially Japan and China. In a recent conference, Russian President Vladimir Putin declared that the Russian Central Bank should switch their foreign-exchange reserves from the U.S. dollar to gold. And several central banks are diversifying their reserves from the dollar to gold. Any wonder why our dollar is depreciating while gold is soaring? One ounce of gold was selling for $262.00 in 2001. Today, it is selling for $630.00, a 240% appreciation in the course of five years. Warren Buffet, the second wealthiest man in the world, is short on the dollar.

What amazes me and lots of other concerned citizens is that there is absolutely no signal from the administration about the calamity we are facing. The President can certainly encourage Americans to use discretion when it comes to buying foreign goods. If we need to buy a foreign car, let us buy a used Mercedes, or Toyota or Lexus. Do not import a new one. When it comes to alcohol, we have the best selection of domestic beers and wines from California.

The President can ask the American people to become discreet in their foreign goods buying for the next 3 years. I pick a three-year period arbitrarily. Would a disciplined spending during the next 3 years reduce the trade deficit? Yes!

In fact, it can bring it down to reasonable levels. More importantly, the discipline exercised in spending during these three years may induce some Americans to continue it for another three or more years, while at the same time they may start saving and reducing the debt on their credit cards. It is a win-win situation.

However, it has to come from our leaders, especially from President Bush.

The second head of the dragon represents our budget deficit. This year's budget is set for a record deficit of $423 billion. Why? Careless spending from our elected officials. They claim the war. There was no war in 2001. There was no war in 2002. We invaded Iraq in 2003. The Bush administration has placed our country into a $2.77 trillion cumulative deficit since they took office back in 2001. Some administrative heads claim Katrina. We are going to have our share of hurricanes every year. You cannot fight Mother Nature. Previous administrations had their share of hurricanes, but they didn't place the nation into trillions of dollars of debt. It appears that deficit spending has become a habit for our government. It needs to be stopped before it is too late. A "bridge to nowhere" in Alaska can be delayed. It should be delayed. It must be delayed. This is just an example of the hundreds of pork projects included in our appropriation bills. And President Bush has yet to veto a bill.

By the time President Bush leaves office in 2008, our cumulative budget deficit under his administration will reach over $4 trillion. That is a conservative estimate. That will be his legacy, the President who has spent more than any other President in the nation's history. This is not a record to be proud of. There is still time to correct this fiscal anomaly, if he becomes decisive and takes the proper steps.

The American public, in general, is not aware of the tremendous power of a trillion. For the sake of my readers, please allow me to extract some passages from the book *A Trillion* written years ago by the Bostonian mathematician Isaac Asimov who was better known for his science fiction writings. In that book, he presents two examples to illustrate the difference between a million and a trillion.

He states that the island of Manhattan is slightly less than one million inches from top to bottom. Question: What kind of a territory would one cover with a trillion inches? The answer is astounding. With a trillion inches one could go 634 times around the world and he will have enough left over to take a trip to the moon and come back to earth. That's the power of a trillion.

His second example deals with time. He states that one million seconds are equal to eleven and a half days. Question: How much time would one cover with a trillion seconds? Again truly astounding. One trillion seconds equals to 31,700 years. In other words, one trillion second ago, dinosaurs were roaming the earth.

Having said that, I am dismayed to find our politicians debate and approve appropriations running into hundreds of billions of dollars without the respective revenue to back up such expenditures. Who is going to pay the difference? That's the question we, our children and our grandchildren will be facing for years to come.

As if this writing of mine wasn't alarming enough, please allow me to paint a scenario which President Bush and his administration will be facing before he leaves office. Let us start with Iraq. We will be in Iraq well after President Bush's departure from office. Therefore, for the next two years he has to play an act on high wire, without a safety net underneath. He needs to be awfully careful in his decision making. Any blunder will have disastrous results.

Next comes Iran. It can safely be stated that Iran will play its energy card rather cunningly, shooting oil prices to new levels, especially after the recent Nigerian conflict between government forces and militia. On top of that, there remains the issue of developing nuclear weapons in the foreseeable future.

Next comes Israel, which in all honesty cannot allow a nuclear-capable, oil-rich enemy like Iran to wipe them off the map. It is unknown how the nuclear delivery systems have been perfected so far. Israel cannot afford to wait. They will strike and strike soon and decisively.

Which places the Bush administration in a precarious position. Chances are Israel will seek assistance and approval from the States. Chances are equally strong that the United States will seek alliances for the need to attack Iran over this issue. Which makes chances even stronger that a deep penetrating nuclear weapon will be needed to take out underground nuclear facilities in Iran. The result will be a big mess in the Middle East with Hamas waiting on the sidelines as for the right opportunity to take their final shot at Israel.

It is my sincere desire and hope that history will record my scenario false and improbable. At any rate, please join me in wishing President Bush all the wisdom in the world, for he will need it. He is about to sign a new bill, just approved by the Senate with a 52-48 vote, raising the nation's debt limit for the fourth time in five years to $9 trillion. Never in our entire history has the debt reached $9 trillion. It is an unimaginable, unthinkable figure. Not our grandchildren but their grandchildren will be unable to pay it off.

Last week, after denouncing the "wayward path" of deficit spending to a group of 2,000 Republican Party supporters, Senator Bill Frist, the Senate majority leader and would-be presidential candidate, was busy presiding over business as usual in the Senate voting for the $9 trillion bill. The Indians have a saying: "You speak with a forked tongue." That's precisely what the doctor from Tennessee is doing.

Senator Frist has voted for every major spending increase and tax cut backed by President Bush since 2001. As the Senate majority leader for more than three years, he bears even greater responsibility than his colleagues for the nation's dismal fiscal condition. Yet, in his speeches, he is calling for greater budget restraint while he is pursuing reckless policies. If this is not a "forked tongue," I don't know what it is.

Other presidential hopefuls like Senators George Allen and John McCain are coming out forcefully as fiscal disciplinarians and yet their voting records do not support their statements.

The swing from a $236 billion surplus in 2000 to a $423 billion deficit today is a huge deterioration in the nation's fiscal balance. A real deficit-reduction plan would call for a return to the budget rules in effect from 1990 to 2000. These "pay-as-you-go" rules helped create the budget surpluses in the 1900's by forcing Congress to pay for both tax cuts and entitlement spending. An effort to reinstate the rules was defeated in the Senate, as recently as last week, with 50 Republicans, including Frist and Allen refusing to reinstate the rules.

For all their recent talk and speeches across the country on wasteful spending, none of the Republican Senators and presidential hopefuls have offered a specific plan for deficit reduction. They keep on voting for more deficit spending while preaching otherwise. If this is not "speaking with a forked tongue," I don't know what is. Let us wake up and cast our votes this coming November for candidates who have common sense, who tell the truth and who are determined to improve on our nation's fiscal policies.

BIOGRAPHY

Born in Istanbul, Turkey. At the age of 7 became an orphan by losing his mother to cancer. The following two years were harsh as he was shuffled from aunt to aunt, until his father remarried.

Following graduation from elementary school, he was admitted to English High School for Boys and thereafter his entire education has been in English. At the age of 20 he was drafted by the Turkish Army, by virtue of his birthplace, and served two years in the army, the last eighteen months as an English interpreter to Brigadier General Resit Ertegun, Supreme Commander of Istanbul.

In 1957 he married Alice, whom he knew from young age, and the following year they embarked on an extensive honeymoon trip around the world. In October of 1958 they arrived in New York and the honeymoon trip had to be interrupted on the advice of the doctors because of Alice's pregnancy to their first child. They never left. However, this was also the beginning of their troubles with the Immigration and Naturalization Service.

The struggle with INS lasted six years, until they became permanent residents thanks to the intervention of Senator Jacob Javitz, Congressman John V. Lindsay and Governor Nelson Rockefeller. On March 26, 1970, Alice and Jim became American citizens.

Jim spent 36 years in the life insurance industry, starting as an agent with New York Life and retiring as a Regional Vice President with John Hancock. Today, he is the President of Stathis Group, Inc., an investment and real estate managing company, which keeps both Alice and Jim busy and young.

Index

978-0-595-41515-1
0-595-41515-6